The Psychology of Nationalism

THE
PSYCHOLOGY
OF
NATIONALISM

Joshua Searle-White

palgrave

First published 2001 by
PALGRAVE™
175 Fifth Avenue, New York, N.Y. 10010 and
Houndmills, Basingstoke, Hampshire, England RG21 6XS.
Companies and representatives throughout the world.

PALGRAVE™ is the new global publishing imprint of St. Martin's Press LLC Scholarly and Reference Division and Palgrave Publishers Ltd (formerly Macmillan Press Ltd).

ISBN 0-312-23369-8 hardback

Library of Congress Cataloging-in-Publication Data

Searle-White, Joshua.
The psychology of nationalism / by Joshua Searle-White.
    p. cm.
Includes bibliographical references and index.
ISBN 0-312-23299-3
1. Nationalism—Psychological aspects. I. Title.

JC311.S415 2001
320.54—dc21   2001032791

A catalogue record for this book is available
from the British Library.

Design by Westchester Book Compostion.

First edition: October, 2001
10 9 8 7 6 5 4 3 2 1

Printed in the United States of America.

CONTENTS

LIST OF MAPS

PREFACE

As part of the research for this book, I traveled to Azerbaijan and went to a refugee camp in the dusty town of Sabirabad, about three hours from Baku. Ten thousand people live in this camp, crowded into tents and tiny mud-brick houses. There is virtually no employment for the refugees, and very little to do; most of the refugees told me that they simply "sit" for most of the day. I wandered from house to house, hearing at each stop the many stories of atrocities that the refugees said were inflicted upon them by Armenians as the Azerbaijanis were forced out of their traditional homes in the disputed territory of Nagorno-Karabakh. The grimness of the refugees' situation was striking and depressing. And then, as I walked back to the entrance to the camp, I heard music. It turned out that I was there on the last day of the school year, and the traditional year-end celebration for graduating high school seniors had just begun. I was ushered into the spare hall where the celebration was taking place. And despite the heat, despite the poverty, and despite the lack of hope that these new graduates must feel when looking at their employment prospects, the young people were having a party. A band played with great enthusiasm into microphones at the front of the hall; tables were laid with soft drinks, marinated and roasted meat, and grape leaves filled with lamb; and the graduates, dressed in elegant black clothes, were dancing around the room. The scene was very amazing and inspiring; in the midst of a desperate and hopeless situation, these people were full of life and promise.

Almost exactly a week later I found myself at another school party, this time in a small village in Armenia, on the other side of the battle lines of the conflict that had placed the Sabirabad refugees into their camp. Here the celebration was to honor an elementary school building that had recently been renovated with the help of the United Nations High Commission on Refugees and a Catholic relief agency. Here, the scene was strikingly similar. A band played with great enthusiasm into microphones at the front of the hall (this time with a clarinet playing lead instead of a guitar); tables were laid with soft drinks, roasted meat, and grape leaves filled with lamb. The teachers from the school were dressed in their best clothes and were dancing around the room. The children from the school performed a number of songs and skits, while the band's keyboard player, who was also the music teacher for the school, directed them and looked at them with eyes so full of love that it was almost palpable. There was life here, too. In this poor village, partly inhabited by Armenians who had had to flee from their homes in Azerbaijan during the war, the teachers and students glowed with vitality and passion and intelligence.

As I was sitting and listening to the music, I happened to think back on the Sabirabad camp. And as I remembered my experience there, I began to feel more and more uncomfortable. Though there are many differences between the Armenian and Azerbaijani peoples (such as religion, economic structures, and history), all those differences somehow began to seem trivial to me. The food was the same. The dancing was the same. The human conditions of their lives, in which children were growing up around adults who cared for them and taught them and wanted the best for them, were the same. Of course, I knew enough to understand the political and historical disputes that had led to war between these peoples, but I could not help being irritated and angry at what seemed to be the futility of it all. From an outsider's point of view, all of these people, who were trying to find ways to have full and satisfying lives in the midst of difficult situations, seemed, in all important ways, indistinguishable. Yet they are enemies, arrayed on two sides of a conflict that shows no immediate signs of ending. The death and destruction that has accompanied the war has swept up both combatants and noncombatants alike, affecting all of their lives. I wanted to know why they were doing this. What do people *as individuals* get out of engaging in such a conflict?

This book is about trying to understand why we humans so often find ourselves in destructive conflict. From the outside, nationalist conflicts like this one can seem so pointless; we are tempted to scream, "Why can't you just get along?" And yet nationalist conflicts are not at all pointless to those who are involved. There are powerful psychological reasons to feel an attachment to a people and to a cause, reasons powerful enough to justify injury or death in their service. And those reasons are common to all of us, not just to people engaged in conflicts in far-off places. My purpose in writing this book is to examine this human side of nationalism. My hope is that the understanding we gain will help us to develop the compassion and the skills needed to make our human interactions less destructive.

ACKNOWLEDGEMENTS

I would like to thank a number of people who have helped with this project directly and indirectly over the past several years. In particular, two mentors, James Wertsch and Richard Ortega, taught me by example about intellectual and personal integrity and about focusing one's efforts on what is most important. I would like to think that their influence can be seen in this work.

Thanks go to William DeLamarter for many conversations that I hope have helped me, in his words, to "finally learn something about social psychology." Bryan Stark, Frank Hoare, Richard Ortega, Michael Peters, Reed Searle, and Barbara Searle gave me helpful comments on a draft of the manuscript. Thanks also go to Ken Achenbach for creating the maps; to Cynthia Burton and Linda Ernst for speedy handling of my unending requests for Interlibrary Loan documents; to Rick Holmgren, Lloyd Michaels, and the Academic Support Committee for supporting my research travel; and to Shawn Meredith for his research assistance in Sri Lanka. I have also received a great deal of inspiration from the students in my Psychology of Nationalism courses over the past several years, whom I will identify by their group names: Arcadia, the Ladybugs Plus One, the Quadlings, Athena's Passage, Group Yo, Hot Jambalaya, Access Denied, Three Girls and a Guy, the Smooth Operators, Styxx, and the Gatekeepers. Their energy and their enthusiasm for group interactions still live on, as do their photographs, which can be found at the following internet address: http://webpub.allegheny.edu/employee/j/jsearle/courses/courselist.html

I would also like to thank the many people who helped me with my research travel. Ovsanna Tadevosian was invaluable in arranging interviews and helping me find my way in Yerevan, and Ruzanna Tadevosian showed me true generosity and hospitality. In Baku, Larry Held, Nadir Guluzadeh, and the staff of the Academy for Educational Development office helped me immeasurably in getting myself oriented, and Anar Jahangirov gave me the benefit of his cultural understanding and his interpreting skills. Rohan Gunaratna has been generous with his support and advice over the past several years, as I have learned about Sri Lanka, and Malinda Seneviratne helped with his excellent interpreting in Kandy and the Nuwara Eliya district. I would also like to thank those many individuals I interviewed in Azerbaijan, Armenia, and Sri Lanka. They may not necessarily agree with what I have to say, but I have tried to use their thoughts and insights as honestly as possible in the service of greater mutual understanding.

On a more personal note, I would also like to thank my parents, Barbara and Reed Searle, for their lifelong support, and my wife, Lisbet, and my daughters, Rachel and Emily; you are in my thoughts and my heart always.

CASPIAN SEA

RUSSIAN FEDERATION

AZERBAIJAN

Baku

Stepanakert/
Khankendi

Nagorno-
Karabakh

Lachin

IRAN

GEORGIA

ARMENIA

Yerevan

Nakhchivan
(Azerbaijan)

TURKEY

Under Armenian Control

0   60 miles

ARMENIA AND AZERBAIJAN

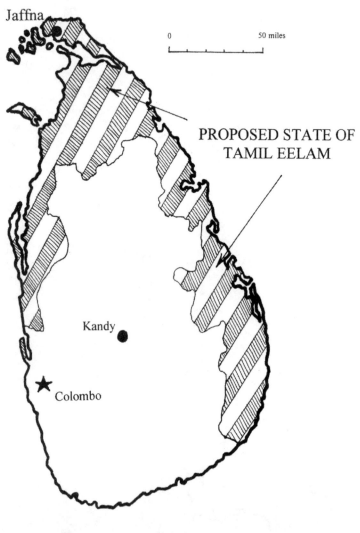

Jaffna

0   50 miles

PROPOSED STATE OF
TAMIL EELAM

Kandy

Colombo

SRI LANKA

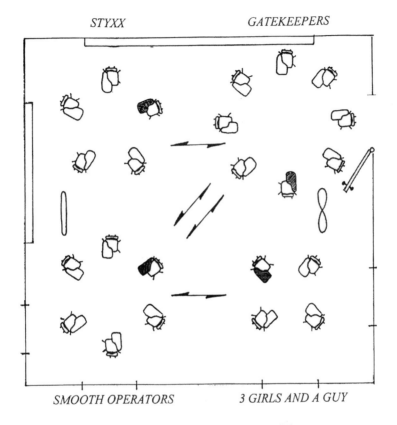

STYXX GATEKEEPERS

SMOOTH OPERATORS 3 GIRLS AND A GUY

Psychology of Nationalism Classroom

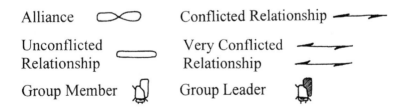

Alliance ⬮⬮

Conflicted Relationship ➤

Unconflicted Relationship ⬭

Very Conflicted Relationship ➤➤

Group Member ▯

Group Leader ▮

INTRODUCTION

The Gatekeepers

On the first day of "group work" in my Psychology of Nationalism course, the students entered to find that the classroom had been divided into four sections by lines of masking tape on the floor. Each section had a set of chairs and a set of colored tent cards with students' names on them. On one of the chairs in each section sat a baseball cap. I explained to the students that they would work in these four groups for the semester. Each group would have a leader, who would wear the baseball cap. The areas marked out on the floor were the four groups' territories.

I then set out the rules. To the largest group, whose color was red, I gave a resource. Their area was next to the door, and I told them that during these group work sessions they had exclusive power over that door—only with their permission could anyone from another group enter or leave the room. Then I gave the four groups their first task. Each group was going to have to do a presentation during the semester, on one of four dates. Some of these dates were better than others. The first task for the groups was to send their leaders into negotiations to decide which group would get which presentation date.

So the leaders of the groups met in the center of the room at the intersection of the four territories. Three of the groups had sent their leaders up with first, second, third, and fourth choices for dates, with instructions to negotiate for the best solution. But not the group that had control over the door. Its members quickly chose the name "the Gatekeepers" and the slogan "If you want to roll, you gotta pay the toll." They sent their leader up to say that they had one choice of date (the most desirable one), and that they were going to take it no matter what the other groups thought. In the negotiations that followed, the Gatekeepers were so obstinate, so uncompromising, and so arrogant that they completely destroyed any chance of a cooperative process. The other groups were furious. The Gatekeepers themselves, however, were having a great time. They were smirking, laughing, and urging their leader to be more and more stubborn, while the other three groups got more and more frustrated and more and more angry.

Ultimately, the Gatekeepers got the date they wanted. And as the semester went on, they continued to be involved in conflicts. They gained a reputation for being difficult; when I asked the groups to write descriptions of each other later in the semester, the Gatekeepers were described by the other groups as "obnoxious, conniving, and greedy"; "volatile with a need for dominance"; "set in their ways, determined, unified—and they don't play well with others."

Obviously, these four groups were not "nationalists" in the sense that they did not have a shared ethnicity, culture, or history. The members of the Gatekeepers had only recently met. They had some "territory," but it was just a patch of classroom floor, and as soon as the class was over it would not belong to them any more. They had a resource—the door—but it was as yet unclear what that was worth, since typically no one needed to enter or leave the room while class was in session. I had also distributed the students relatively randomly (except that there were more men in the Gatekeepers group than in any of the others), so as to reduce the potential effects of individual personalities on the interactions. The issues involved were completely trivial and manufactured by the classroom situation.

Yet putting these students into this situation produced something quite akin to nationalism. The Gatekeepers developed a clear sense of group identity. They felt proud of their name and their symbol (a doorway, covered over by bars, with a large gold key superimposed over the center), and they all wore red (their "official" group color) during each group session. They enjoyed the feeling of group cohesiveness that very quickly arose, and that intensified each time they humiliated or defeated the other groups. Beginning in that first session and continuing throughout the semester, they sought to promote themselves, to maximize their own gains, and to disparage the efforts of others. And the resulting emotions were very real. In many ways, the Gatekeepers seemed to portray many attitudes and behaviors that are seen in nationalist conflicts. It seems to be very easy to create group identities and intergroup hostility, even in a setting where the differences between the groups are minimal and arbitrary.

The Psychological Dimensions of Nationalism

Obviously, nationalist conflicts in the real world are much more serious and much more complex than this classroom exercise. Territory, political control, and human lives are at stake. There are economic, historical, and geopolitical realities that help shape the way conflicts arise and are fought. Nations fight over resources; poor people enter into military service because they have little chance for alternative employment; nearby powers might provoke conflicts on their borders to secure their influence there. But nationalism is more than just "nations" interacting. Nationalism involves individuals, people who *engage* in nationalism, who carry strong attitudes and beliefs about their own people and about others, who feel their attachment to their nation passionately, and who even, at times, act with great cruelty against their enemies. Nationalist conflicts are increasingly common around the world today, and they are often brutal and tenacious. The violence of nationalist conflicts often goes far beyond what would be needed simply to capture territory or to secure resources. This book is about the psychological dimensions of nationalism—those human qualities that make it so easy for us to identify with a nation, to act on its behalf, and to engage in nationalist conflict with others. And it is about why, once we have engaged in a conflict, it is often so difficult for us to let it go.

An Inherent Tension

Nationalism, in its broadest definition (the one I will use here), is simply a sense of identification with a group of people who share a common history, language, territory, culture, or some combination of these. Nationalism may or may not explicitly be a movement to create an independent state for a national group, although, because self-determination is privileged in the world today, the nation-state (an independent country that is populated primarily by one national group) is a particular goal of many nationalist movements. Nationalism today has a particular urgency because, although it does not necessarily *have* to lead to violent conflict, it often does.

Trying to understand the psychological aspects of nationalism and nationalist conflict leads to an inherent tension. The intent of this book is to identify the thoughts, feelings, and actions that underlie our attachment to national groups. On the one hand, those psychological processes are shaped by individual experience and cultural context. A person who has lost a family member to a pogrom will likely feel differently about the group who carried out the pogrom than will a person who has not. A member of a small and disenfranchised minority will likely experience nationalism differently than will a member of a majority group in a powerful country. Nationalism does not happen in a vacuum; individuals engage in nationalist movements in particular times and places. On the other hand, studying the psychological aspects of nationalism at all presumes that there is something common among widely disparate peoples, from Quebecois agitating for secession from Canada to Azerbaijanis hoping to reclaim Nagorno-Karabakh. And indeed, we are all human, and that commonality means that we all need to struggle with some of the very same issues, such as developing relationships, living meaningful lives, and facing the possibility of death. The story of the psychological dimensions of nationalism can thus only be told within the tension between, on the one hand, the language, culture, history, and social context of particular peoples, and, on the other hand, the universal psychological processes that are part of being human.

There are two ways to work through this tension. First, I will use the concept of "identity" as a thread to tie the discussion together. Our identity, or sense of who we are, has two sources.[1] The first is our own individual history, the unique set of perceptions and experiences we have each had in life. The second is our affiliation with groups, and particularly national groups, including our evaluation of how those groups have fared, what they have done, and how others view them. Identity is thus simultaneously individual and social, and our national identity is as much a part of us as is our own individual history. Because identity is simultaneously individual and social, it links up the experiences of individuals with the contextual factors so important in understanding nationalism. In particular, I will argue that because of the nature of identity, we as humans are primed to feel threatened; and that our perception of our identity's fragility is what leads us into nationalist conflicts and violence. I should note briefly here that national identity is only one kind of group identity. Nationalism is the focus here because national identity is prized as a way of gaining respect and legitimacy in today's world. As I describe in chapter 3, ethnic, religious, and class identity can serve similar functions and have in other historical periods.

Second, I will examine the psychological dynamics of nationalism in the context of two ongoing nationalist conflicts. Actual conflicts embody both the universality and the particularity of nationalism, and they provide a way to see how psychological dynamics are played out in the real world. The two conflicts are that between Armenia and Azerbaijan, and that between the government of Sri Lanka and a separatist group known as the Liberation Tigers of Tamil Eelam (LTTE).

Nagorno-Karabakh is an Armenian-populated region within the territory of Azerbaijan, on the southern edge of the Caucasus. As the Soviet Union began to fall apart in 1988, Nagorno-Karabakh declared its independence from Azerbaijan and its intention to unite with Armenia. An increasingly violent conflict ensued involving troops from Armenia, Nagorno-Karabakh, and Azerbaijan, as well as the Soviet troops in the area. By the time a ceasefire was established in 1994, perhaps 15,000 people had died[2]; in addition, riots, expulsions, and population exchanges had created a refugee crisis, with more than half a million refugees living in camps in Azerbaijan alone.[3] The conflict remains unresolved, and ethnic Armenian troops currently control nearly 20 percent of Azerbaijan.[4]

Sri Lanka is a small island nation located off the southern coast of India. The Sri Lankan government, which is dominated by the majority Sinhalese, is facing a secessionist threat by the LTTE, who claim to represent the Tamil minority that historically lives in the north and east of the island. The government, while offering substantial devolution of power to the north and east, insists upon the territorial integrity of the country. The LTTE is advocating a separate state for the Tamils, on the grounds that the Sri Lankan Tamils are a separate and unique people and that they must have a state to protect them from the majority Sinhalese. Each group has substantial grievances against the other, including terrorism and violence by the armed forces on each side[5] and periodic ethnic riots, primarily by Sinhalese against Tamils.[6] As of early 2001, more than 60,000 people have died in this conflict,[7] and many others, particularly Tamils, have fled to countries around the world.

These two conflicts share some similarities. Both conflicts deal with separatism, and both have led to violent confrontations, with tragic results, including thousands of dead and wounded and many more thousands of refugees. In both, there are religious differences; Christian and Muslim in the Armenia-Azerbaijan case, and Buddhist and Hindu in the Sri Lankan case. In both areas there is a history of foreign control. For the Armenians and Azeris, it was the Soviet Union; both became part of the U.S.S.R. in 1923 and left it in 1991. Sri Lanka was colonized by the Portuguese and then the British, with substantial consequences for both Tamil and Sinhalese identity. In both cases one of the groups has a significant overseas diaspora (the Armenians and the Tamils) that raises money and provides other means of support for its independence movement. And both areas lie within the spheres of influence of much larger powers, namely Russia and India.

There are also many differences between the conflicts. The Armenians see themselves as a Christian enclave surrounded by Muslims (in Azerbaijan, Turkey, and Iran), whereas the Tamils in Sri Lanka are not far from a large number of Tamils in India; the Buddhists in Sri Lanka are a majority in their country and a minority in the region. The Armenia-Azerbaijan conflict is currently at a stalemate, with little or no current violence. Sri Lanka's conflict, at this writing, is still continuing, with high levels of violence and social disruption.

This broad spectrum of historical, religious, and political contexts mirrors the many settings in which nationalist conflict is taking place in the world today. To explore the psychological dynamics underlying the two conflicts described above, I will weave together a range of research and thinking from psychology and related fields, together with published commentaries about these conflicts, and interviews that I conducted in visits to those two regions. In addition, as a way of highlighting the universality of the psychological processes underlying nationalism, I will also describe some of the incidents that happened in my Psychology of Nationalism course. Overall, these various settings will provide concrete illustrations of the universal psychological processes I will discuss.

The Main Point of the Book

The ultimate intent of this book is to provide a window into the psychological dynamics of nationalist conflict, so that interventions can better reduce its destructive effects. Nationalism is not inherently evil; indeed, devotion to a nation can bring out transcendent qualities in people, facilitating selflessness, courage, and idealism. Yet its destructive effects are obvious throughout the world; and the losses—in life, suffering, property, and dignity—are often staggering, particularly since the victims of nationalist conflict are often noncombatants who are targeted simply because of who they are. To the extent that nationalist conflict is tied up with identity, resolving it, or at least managing it, requires sophistication in dealing with identity issues. This book will use the psychological insights developed here to suggest concrete intervention strategies for conflict for all those who are involved.

Perhaps more important, however, is a more basic point. It may be tempting to think of nationalism and nationalist conflict as something that "others" engage in, while "we," at a distance, are somehow immune to such problems. However, we all identify with a variety of groups; we all sometimes feel threat; we all act on the basis of our feelings and experiences; and we all get into conflicts that can be destructive. My hope is that each reader will recognize in him- or herself the same feelings, the same desires, and the same fears that I will describe as underlying nationalism. Our own experiences can help us to understand the difficulty in giving up conflict and in tolerating the feelings that drive us into nationalism. If we let go of the illusion that "we" are different from "them," we will take the first step in being able to understand nationalism fully.

Thus the study presented here is offered as a window looking outward to the world of nationalism, but also looking inward, toward our own experience. It is intended to give those in conflict—that is, potentially, all of us—more ways to preserve dignity and identity without engaging in destructive conflict.

Chapter 1

WHAT WE KNOW ABOUT NATIONALISM

Psychologists, as a whole, have studied nationalism only sporadically.[1] However, there is a great deal of psychological research that describes how we categorize people, how we think about ourselves and about others, and how we tend to act when we get into groups. Looking at this research, we will find that people act in predictable ways that predispose us to group together and to engage in conflict.

Categorizing

The first observation that psychology has made is that the very way our minds work—the way we process information—shapes the way we feel about ourselves and about others. The fundamental process that begins this chain of events is categorizing. Categorizing, of course, is essential for us to make our way through life. If we did not categorize, we would need to investigate each and every new object or idea we came in contact with. If I am about to cross a road and see a large, ten-wheeled object moving toward me at a great rate of speed, I categorize it as dangerous and I move out of the way. If I were to spend the time to investigate it in detail, I might well get run over before I am finished! Categorizing allows us to deal with life's uncertainties more efficiently.[2]

On what basis do we categorize ourselves? In nationalism, the situation is much more complex than it might initially seem. There are a number of potential characteristics that people might use in classifying themselves into national groups. In the case of my Psychology of Nationalism class, the Gatekeepers knew who was who because each group had its own part of the classroom and its own list of members. They did not have to share any common history, language, or culture; the members of each group were, in a sense, "citizens" of their group simply by virtue of "owning" that territory, by living within it and following the same group rules. Indeed, much of nationalism in Western Europe and North America defines the "nation" by where a person lives. If someone moves to the United States, for example, he or she can become an "American" by living in the United States and acculturating, following its laws and customs. By U.S. law, anyone born in the United States becomes an American citizen. So one way to define who is part of a nation is to think about nationality essentially as "citizenship," wherein belonging to a national group comes from living in a particular area and being a part of its political community and civic structure.[3]

Another way to determine who is a member of a national group is to focus not on territory but on lineage, language, and religion—what has been called an "ethnic" idea of national identity.[4] In Armenia and Azerbaijan, for example, the two groups come from different descent, speak different languages (Armenian and Azerbaijani), and profess different religions (Armenian Orthodox and Shiite Muslim). In Sri Lanka, the Sinhalese and Tamils come from different descent, speak different languages (Tamil and Sinhalese), and belong primarily to different religions (Hindu and Theravada Buddhist). Interestingly, in Sri Lanka, ethnic heritage is seen as an important factor in distinguishing Tamils from Sinhalese, even though it may be illusory. The claim is often made that the Sinhalese are of Aryan (North Indian) descent, while the Tamils are of Dravidian (South Indian) descent. There are differences between the languages that would seem to support this claim, but recently scholars have noted that it may well be that many of those in Sri Lanka today who identify themselves as Sinhalese may in fact come from south Indian (and even Tamil) roots.[5] The reality of the distinction is less important than the perception. If a group believes that it is very different from another group, that is enough for all of the cognitive processes described in this chapter to develop.

These groups exemplify more of the "ethnic" conception of nationhood. However, we need to be careful about applying these distinctions too broadly. In addition to the broad distinction between national groups just mentioned, there are many distinctions *within* groups that at times may also be very important. For example, most Sinhalese are Buddhist, and most

Tamils are Hindu. However, there are many Sinhalese and Tamil Christians, as well as a small community of Muslims (known as "Moors," many of them Tamil-speaking),[6] and so religion alone (except in the case of the Muslims) is not sufficient to distinguish the groups. In addition, in Sri Lanka, shared cultural and social history also plays a role. Those who live in Sri Lanka make a distinction between Sri Lankan Tamils (who live primarily in the north and east of Sri Lanka and have lived on the island for many centuries) and the "Indian" or "plantation" Tamils, who were brought to Sri Lanka in the nineteenth century by the British to work on coffee and tea plantations in the south central highlands.[7] Both groups are Tamils, with the same language and religion, but their consciousness of themselves is very different due to their different histories on the island.[8] As will be seen later, that difference in consciousness will have a large effect on the participation of Sri Lankan and Indian Tamils in the nationalist movement in Sri Lanka.

In Armenia and Azerbaijan the situation is also complex. In the past there were many Azerbaijanis living on the territory of the Armenian Soviet Socialist Republic. However, even if they learned Armenian or lived in that area for generations, they would never be considered Armenians. Soviet internal passports listed one's nationality (determined by the nationalities of one's parents), distinct from one's citizenship (Soviet) and where one lived. Similarly, members of a variety of national groups, such as Lezghins, Kurds, and Talish, live in present-day Azerbaijan. Though they are citizens of Azerbaijan, they are not Azerbaijanis. However, at the same time, there are many ethnic Azerbaijanis living in Iran who conceive of themselves as Azerbaijanis.[9] And there are many members of the Armenian diaspora who have grown up in Lebanon, Fresno, or the many other centers of Armenian culture in the world. Even if they do not speak Armenian, they still could easily call themselves Armenians and feel a true kinship to the Armenian people.[10]

Hence there are different ways to classify ourselves into national groups. Which dimension will be most salient—and at what time, and in which situation—can change, as will be discussed in chapter 4. For now, the most important thing to understand is that no matter what intergroup boundaries exist, they are still associated with predictable attitudes and thinking patterns. This is as true whether the distinction is between very large groups (Tamils and Sinhalese) or much smaller ones (Karabakh Armenians and Yerevan Armenians). Categorization forms the foundation of how we think about national groups.

Attitudes Toward Ingroups and Outgroups

Once we conceive of ourselves as being in different national groups, we tend to develop predictable patterns of attitudes toward ourselves and others. To begin with, people tend to see the members of their group (the "ingroup") as good, moral, and strong.[11] Social psychologists have termed this process "ingroup favoritism."[12] These observations are supported by ethnographic data from societies in various areas of the world,[13] and indeed it would seem natural to think that our own group, the people we know and identify with, is better than others. Interestingly, though, even when groups are created artificially and based on minimal real differences, such as in laboratory research, people still tend to favor their ingroup. In one study, participants were divided into groups supposedly on the basis of what kinds of photographs they liked. (The division into groups was actually random.) When the participants were asked to describe the personality traits of the members of their group and the other group, they rated their own group more positively than the other one, even though they had no common experience or history together.[14] Similar findings have arisen in many variations on this study.[15]

Obviously, it does not take much looking to find examples of ingroup favoritism in everyday life. High schools, religious organizations, sports teams, and many other groups do the same thing. Being a saxophone player myself, I have always believed that saxophonists are superior to other woodwind players (not to mention the brass and string players!).

National groups are no different. In discussions with Karabakh Armenians[16], I was told that they are: strong and brave; proud and outspoken; and the best fighters in the region (never having submitted to invaders and, in fact, having protected other Armenians at various times in history). Several people mentioned that all four of the Armenian marshals of the U.S.S.R. (the highest military rank in the Soviet Army) and 25 Heroes of the U.S.S.R. (one of the two highest awards given in the Soviet Union), were from Karabakh. In fact, after listing these various distinctions, one man even went on to suggest jokingly that perhaps Karabakh Armenians discovered America!

The tendency to describe one's own group more favorably than a rival group, then, is common, and it seems to flow naturally from categorization. However, along with the tendency to favor one's ingroup, we also tend to think in predictable ways about outgroups. First, we tend to describe the outgroup as though all members in it were the same. One of the most complete discussions of this topic is found in a classic book by Gordon Allport called *The Nature of Prejudice*. Allport notes that a category tends to "saturate all that it contains with the same ideational and emotional flavor."[17] That is, once we classify someone as part of a national group, we will tend to believe that he or she has all the same qualities as the others in the group. The way we feel about that group will then color the way we feel about that individual.[18]

A striking example of this phenomenon (termed "outgroup homogenization") came when one supporter of the Karabakh cause in Armenia described the Azerbaijanis by saying:

> Turks are Turks. The nation is fanatical. They will follow any bestial order from their leaders—they will do anything.

To this speaker, the Azerbaijanis are simply Turks, and Turks are all alike. This characterization is not limited to this one person; Azerbaijanis whom I interviewed reported often being called "Turks" when they were growing up in Nagorno-Karabakh. It is true that the Azerbaijanis and the Turks are linguistically and ethnically closely related. Azerbaijanis sometimes call themselves "Azeri Turks," in contrast to the "Ottoman Turks" who live in present-day Turkey. Nonetheless, the two groups have very different historical and religious (Shiite versus Sunni Muslim) differences between them; in addition, not all Turks are alike. But the truth or falsity of the characterization is not the issue. Allport would suggest that if a person believes that all Azerbaijanis and Turks are alike, then it is likely that the person would have similar feelings and attitudes toward all of those people. In this case, if the speaker believes that all Azerbaijanis are the same as Turks, then he might well blame the Azerbaijanis for the massacres of Armenians in Turkey in 1915—and, as we will see later, this belief in turn could have a strong influence on why he believes the war over Nagorno-Karabakh is justified.

Stereotypes

Stereotypes are the result of categorization and outgroup homogenization. A stereotype is simply a generalization presumed to hold true about a group of people. What is most important for understanding nationalism is that if we hold a stereotype about a group, that stereotype then *shapes* how we understand any new information that we encounter about that group.

For example, the more we think that the members of a national group are alike, the more we are likely to believe that the behavior of one member of the group characterizes all of them.[19] One Azerbaijani refugee told me the following story to illustrate what Armenians are like:

> When I was a child, I went fishing on a small river in Karabakh. I was fishing, and an Armenian man came who wanted to fish there too. He said that if he could fish there, he would "lend" me his wife for the night. That's what Armenians are like. They use their women to get what they want.

Of course, there is no way of assessing this story's credibility; after all, the speaker was someone who had lost his home to the Armenians. However, the truth of the story is not the issue. In this story, the behavior shown by one Armenian is now presumed to characterize all Armenians, and the stereotype is reinforced.

Another major way that stereotypes shape our perception is by affecting our memory for new information. Research has shown that we tend to remember information about groups better if it confirms our already existing beliefs about those groups. In one study, participants were led to believe that a group of men was either friendly or intellectual, and then read a set of behavior descriptions about the group. When tested later to see which of the descriptions they remembered, those participants who believed that the group was friendly remembered descriptions of friendly behavior best; and those who believed that the group was intellectual remembered descriptions of intellectual behavior best. [20] In fact, research also suggests that if we learn information about a person that does *not* fit with our stereotype of his or her group, then we are *less* likely to remember that behavior.[21] In general, we tend to believe positive things about our ingroup and negative things about the outgroup.[22]

An illustration of this phenomenon comes from Sri Lanka. In 1998, the LTTE set off a bomb at the Temple of the Tooth in Kandy, one of the historical capitals of Sri Lanka. The Temple of the Tooth is said to hold a fragment of the Buddha's tooth, and it is one of the most sacred sites in Theravada Buddhism. The bomb that destroyed part of the temple was in a truck, and residents of Kandy who were there told me that the blast could be heard and felt all around the city. Most interesting in the descriptions from some of the residents, however, was the assertion that several hours before the blast, all Tamils in Kandy mysteriously found ways to leave their workplaces, under the guise of family emergencies or the need to take a vacation. Obviously, no terrorist group would alert a large segment of the population in advance of a bomb attack, since that would almost certainly result in the authorities being alerted too. Yet even though the LTTE is composed of only a small number of Tamils, the category "LTTE" seems to be joined with that of "Tamils," and so some Sinhalese residents of Kandy were ready to believe that all Tamils knew about the bomb and left so that only Sinhalese would be hurt by it. In this way, the images we hold about national groups shape our thinking so that new information we receive reinforces those stereotypes.

Our stereotypes also lead us to believe that we are more different from members of other groups than we actually are. Social psychology has explored this tendency in research on attitudes. In a series of studies conducted in 1967 and 1968, people who identified themselves as "hawks" or "doves" with regard to the war in Vietnam were asked to write statements that they thought people in the opposing group would agree with.[23] Overall, each group wrote statements that the other group would not accept because they were simply too extreme. In essence, once the participants were thinking about people who differed from them, they attributed much more extreme attitudes to them than were really the case; they accentuated the differences between them. This process does seem to vary with how strongly a person holds the view in question. In another study conducted in the late 1970s, members of the Boston chapter of the National Organization for Women and the Massachusetts Federation of Republican Women answered a series of questions about women's rights. The researchers found that the more extreme a person's view, the more extreme she judged the views of people in the opposing group to be.[24]

How is this tendency, which psychologists call the "contrast effect," relevant to nationalism? In most cases of nationalism, the central differences between the groups involved would seem to be their culture, language, or history, rather than their attitudes. However, attitudes play a very important role in our images of the outgroup. For example, in one large-scale cross-cultural research study on ethnocentrism, the one attitude that seemed to be universal was that the ingroup is more trustworthy and moral than various outgroups.[25] Combined with the research on attitudes, then, we would expect nationalist groups to perceive other groups as untrustworthy and immoral, and very different. And indeed, the contrast effect could help to create a cycle that might increase group conflict, as one set of researchers suggest:

> To the degree to which [the contrast effect] is strong or prevalent, it will exacerbate the conflict between opposing groups; for if members of each group believe that statements of members of the other group represent more

extreme attitudes than they in fact do, each group will believe it to be more difficult to compromise with the other than it in fact would be; further, the belief that members of the other group hold extreme attitudes will lead to a lowering of esteem for that group, which in turn will strengthen the contrast effect. Thus, this effect is both destructive and self-perpetuating.[26]

So the way we perceive others can intensify a cycle of conflict. As we will see below, the perception of outgroups as untrustworthy will also play significantly into the way in which national groups provide justification for violence and aggression against others.

Outgroup Devaluation

The tendency to think negatively about people in other groups is probably the most obvious ingroup-outgroup phenomenon.[27] Examples of it are easy to find. At the end of the first day of group work in my Psychology of Nationalism course, for example, the leader of the Smooth Operators (another of the student groups) returned to her group and described the Gatekeepers as "a bunch of barbarians." (Of course, she did have some evidence for this description, given their behavior during the class session, but "barbarians" was a bit of an exaggeration.) In Azerbaijan, an Azerbaijani veteran of the Karabakh war and a former resident of Karabakh described the Armenian people by saying:

> Armenians are a vindictive people. Even if it happened in Karabakh that an Azerbaijani somehow killed an Armenian, then the Armenians would kill two or three people in revenge.

In turn, several Armenian interviewees I talked with described the Azerbaijanis, as a people, as very poor fighters and said that their lack of fighting ability is why they lost the Karabakh war. Outgroup devaluation is one of the most predictable of the ingroup-outgroup phenomena, and people in all kinds of group contexts engage in it.

Psychological and anthropological research has identified this process in many different contexts, and it seems to be a natural (though perhaps not inevitable) consequence of categorizing ourselves into national groups. Descriptions could go on almost indefinitely; every national group has other groups that it denigrates in jokes or stories. The importance of outgroup devaluation for nationalism is that once we believe that the enemy is bad or evil, it becomes easy to justify violence and aggression against them.

The Influence of Images and Propaganda

Of course, in nationalist conflict, there are explicit attempts to shape one group's image of the other, also called propaganda. For example, the following appears in a publication obtained from the Azerbaijan Embassy in Washington, D.C.:

> The history evidently shows that leaders of Armenia, [whether] bourgeois, communists or "democrats," . . . demonstrate unanimity in their desire to absorb the lands of their neighbors. . . . It is not the problem of today. [The] Armenian national movement has [. . .] deep roots and in the course of centuries it was being led and directed by the Armenian clergy. . . . Armenian priests take up arms. Maybe the best thing that a priest of [the] Armenian Apostolic Church can do is to show the world laymen in its personal example that killing [the] faithless is really a good deed?[28]

The image of Armenians in this pamphlet is of people who are on a crusade to expand their territory at the expense of their neighbors, inspired by a vicious and nationalist church. This image of a greedy people bent on acquiring territory could play very clearly into the actions of the Azerbaijani people as they think about what to do about the conflict over Nagorno-Karabakh. If the Armenians are in fact attempting to "absorb the lands of their neighbors," then wouldn't all of Azerbaijan be at risk? Given the way that stereotypes shape our perceptions, if Azerbaijanis hold such an image of Armenians, the Azerbaijanis will tend to interpret new information in the light of this preexisting belief.

The images used to describe enemies can be very vivid. Journalist Sam Keen, in a book titled *Faces of the Enemy*,[29] details the characteristics that tend to arise over and over again in propaganda portrayals of enemies. Drawing from war posters from World War II and other conflicts, Keen demonstrates that enemies tend to be portrayed as aggressive, godless, uncivilized, greedy, lawless, sadistic, and misogynistic. In fact, enemies are often frankly dehumanized—characterized as animals: Uncle Sam as a spider creeping across Western Europe; Hitler as a rat, chewing through the Molotov-Ribbentrop Pact; contras in Nicaragua as reptiles with chicken feet; and England as an octopus strangling the world. Such propaganda images can also be verbal, such as in the following description of Sri Lankan Tamil émigrés, from a publication by the Sri Lankan government:

Many expatriate Tamils have helped to create the terrorist monster in the north of Sri Lanka and supported an intensive propaganda campaign directed at establishing charges of massive violations of human rights amounting to genocide by the majority community. It is easy for these "heroes" who enjoy lucrative employment and live in luxury abroad to acclaim northern terrorists as liberation fighters and to heap scorn and insult on the land of their birth. It would be much less easy for these well-heeled expatriates to give up their affluent life styles in exchange for the inclement climate and the barren soils of the Northern Province of Sri Lanka.[30]

The image that this publication presents is one of rich overseas Tamils being armchair cheerleaders for the Tamil cause. By implication, it tars all expatriate Sri Lankan Tamils, not only the ones who support the LTTE. Of course, it cannot be true that all overseas Sri Lankan Tamils are the same, or hold the same views, or are like this portrayal. It is also not true that Hitler was a rat or that the English are octopuses or that all Armenian priests have taken up arms against Azerbaijan. But because of the way that our minds categorize, interpret, and retain information, propaganda like this works.

And indeed, there is evidence that propaganda works, even when it is based on irrelevant associations. In one study, for example, students were asked to make decisions about a hypothetical international crisis. In the materials given to them, there were words that were designed to make the students think of either World War II, such as a briefing room called "Winston Churchill Hall," or of the Vietnam War, such as a reference to civilians fleeing in small boats. The idea was that the associations to World War II would evoke a time when intervention was positive, and the associations to the Vietnam War would evoke a time when intervention was negative. As it turned out, when the students decided whether or not to intervene in a hypothetical crisis, the students who were exposed to the associations to World War II were indeed more likely to intervene in the conflict than those exposed to the associations to the Vietnam War.[31] Here the associations were completely irrelevant to the facts at hand, yet they nonetheless had an influence on the decisions that were made.

Of course, such principles can be used by governments or others to design propaganda. Two researchers recently commented that if the U.S. government could have gotten people to believe that Saddam Hussein was like Adolph Hitler, they would have had an easier time marshalling support for the Persian Gulf War.[32] Propaganda portrayals are effective because they play on the fundamental cognitive and social processes that have been discussed above. They help to define an image of an "other," and once that image is defined, it in turn shapes any new information we obtain.

Stories of Atrocities

One way in which stereotypes, images of the enemy, and mass media all come together in conflict situations is in stories of atrocities committed by the enemy. Such stories are passed from person to person, picked up by the media, and sometimes used explicitly by a nationalist leadership to describe the terrible qualities of the enemy. Although atrocities certainly are committed in most nationalist conflicts, it is often extremely difficult to know for sure whether or not a particular story is true. What is important, however, is that the stories are both a consequence of the way we think about outgroups and a spur for further hostility against those outgroups.

The connection between rumors, stereotypes, and violence has been studied in a number of contexts. In a study of rumors and race riots in the United States over the past 100 years, one researcher, Terry Ann Knopf, identified themes that arose consistently.[33] Among whites, the rumors were primarily of black men raping white women, of black brutality, and of conspiracies by blacks. Among blacks, the most common rumors were of white brutality, police brutality, and conspiracies by whites. Nearly all of the race riots Knopf studied were accompanied by rumors. The rumors were often sparked by actual events, but their real importance was in spurring people to act, either at the beginning of a riot, in the middle of one, or in retaliation after the damage of a riot.

Rumors, particularly of atrocities and brutality, seem to be a persistent feature of war and nationalist conflict. In August and September 1914, German troops crossed through Belgium. Since Belgium was neutral during World War I, the German troops did not expect resistance. However, stories soon began to circulate about so-called *francs tireurs*—Belgians, primarily priests, although often women and children—coming out of hiding and committing atrocities against the soldiers. There were stories, for example, of women pouring boiling water on soldiers as they passed through a village, of women and children sawing the legs off an innocent German soldier, of priests paying people to massacre Germans, of priests cutting the breasts off a Red Cross worker.[34] These stories were accompanied by rumors of Germans cutting the hands off of Belgian babies and leaving them to die.[35] Later investigation turned up evidence that few, if any, of the atrocities by Belgians against the Germans ever took place,[36] and that some of them (such as the story about the Red Cross worker) were consciously fabricated.[37] Yet these events were reported by soldiers and newspapers, and apparently believed even by the German emperor himself. The situation in Armenia and Azerbaijan provides similar examples. In Azerbaijan, refugees from Nagorno-Karabakh told me many stories of atrocities that they believed had been committed by Armenians against Azerbaijanis. Here are examples:

- In Nagorno-Karabakh, Armenian forces occupied the land on one side of a graveyard, while Azerbaijani forces and refugees were on the other. The Azerbaijanis would at times call the Armenians on the radio and ask for permission to come into the graveyard to bury their dead. In one instance, a child from Nagorno-Karabakh lost a member of his family. At the funeral, he came into the grave-yard and hugged the gravestone at the family member's grave. Unfortunately, the side that his hands were on, hugging the grave-stone, was the side that the Armenians were on. They shot at him and the bullet went right through both of his hands, right where they had clasped the gravestone.
- Two Azerbaijani families were fleeing Nagorno-Karabakh in a jeep. They were going through a tunnel, and at the end some Armenians stopped them; the end of the tunnel was near a lake. One of the families had a child who was five months old. The Armenians took the child and threw him in the lake. The mother ran out into the lake, rescued the child, and brought him back to shore. The Arme-nians then threw the child into the lake again. This time, however, as the mother tried to run out and save him, they shot her in the leg so that she couldn't, and the baby drowned. The woman was preg-nant at the time, and due to the shock of being shot, she had a mis-carriage. The woman eventually went crazy.
- Armenians took champagne bottles and rammed them inside Azerbaijani women's vaginas until they were completely inside. The women were then brought back to Baku for medical treat-ment. One doctor in particular, an expert surgeon from Turkey, saw one of these women with a champagne bottle inside her and was so upset that he had a heart attack and died right there.

These stories emphasize brutality, sexual violence, and desecration of women, just as the rumors studied by Knopf did. There is no doubt that atrocities have occurred on both sides in the Armenia-Azerbaijan conflict.

In fact, I was told similar stories by Armenians about atrocities committed by Azerbaijanis. In most cases, however, it is impossible to determine whether or not such atrocities actually occurred, and if so, if they happened the way the stories would suggest. However, while we may not know exactly what happened, we can make some guesses about when rumors tend to arise, how they are transmitted, and how their content might change in the process. Gordon Allport and Leo Postman published a classic psychological treatment of rumors in which they proposed that the intensity of a rumor is determined in a multiplicative fashion—how important the subject is to individuals, *multiplied by* the ambiguity of the information.[38] In discussing this theory, they comment:

> In wartime . . . the conditions for rumor are optimal. Military events are of the greatest importance. Yet military secrecy, together with the natural confusion of a nation on the march, and the unpredictable moves of the enemy, help create profound ambiguity in precisely those matters that are of greatest concern to us.[39]

A situation like the Nagorno-Karabakh conflict fits these criteria. Rumors are most likely to spread in the absence of reliable information[40] and when people have little control over events as they happen.[41] As Allport and Postman note, secrecy and confusion can prevent reliable information from being available. And to compound the situation, Armenia and Azerbaijan used to be part of the Soviet Union, in which distrust of official sources of information was rampant, and the ability to effect individual change in the larger society was minimal. These factors combine to make the Nagorno-Karabakh conflict ideal for the spreading of stories and rumors.

How do such stories evolve? If we disregard deliberate falsehoods and propaganda, the process could happen like this: The story starts as a testimony from an individual. Others hear the story and repeat it.[42] Allport and Postman's research, as well as the work of others after them, has shed some light on what happens in the process of retelling the story. First, as a rumor or story is spread, the minor and unimportant details tend to be lost. The story becomes shorter and more concise. Allport and Postman termed this phenomenon "leveling." Second, the most salient aspects of the story (salient for a particular listener or group, that is) become more prominent, in a phenomenon termed "sharpening." And, most importantly, rumors or stories tend to change so that they fit the beliefs and needs of the listeners, which is termed "assimilation."[43]

In the stories listed above, some of these processes may be at work. In the story of the women being violated with champagne bottles, there are many details that seem to have been leveled out—when the incidents took place, the name of the surgeon, the situation in which the assaults happened. And yet there are several elements that seem to have been sharpened: the identification of the bottles as champagne bottles (rather than any other kind), the nationality of the surgeon (Turkish), and the surgeon's reaction (a heart attack). Why might those elements have been highlighted in the story rather than others? Since we do not know the origin of the story, we do not know the answer. We might guess that the detail about champagne bottles was retained (or inserted into the story) because of their size; they are larger than wine or vodka bottles, and therefore the assaults are that much more horrible. Since Turkey has provided various kinds of expertise to Azerbaijan in recent years, it might be that the association of Turkey with the surgeon has something to do with assimilating the idea of the expertise expected of a doctor with the experience of Turkish specialists in Azerbaijan. The heart attack may be a way of conveying the horror over a sexual atrocity of this kind. At the same time, there may be processes at work that go beyond this particular conflict. Similar accusations about violating women with bottles, as well as cutting open the abdomens of pregnant women, were made in 1954 during the Mau Mau emergency in Kenya.[44] Sexual violence is common in wartime behavior, as I will discuss in more detail in chapter 4, as are stories about the sexual atrocities committed by the enemy.

Overall, these stories are clear and concise. The main points—the particular cruelty of the Armenians' alleged actions—are very sharply defined. How do such stories gain wide currency? First, someone, perhaps a refugee or a soldier, will tell the story. Others hear it and repeat it, with the transmission following the pattern that Allport and Postman describe. Eventually, such stories may be picked up by news organizations which may or may not attempt to verify their origin.[45] One journalist who worked in Azerbaijan during the Nagorno-Karabakh conflict complained that some stories, such as one about Azerbaijanis using the heads of Armenians as soccer balls, gained currency when they should not have.[46] Obviously, checking the sources of stories is important in any news reporting situation, and it does not always happen.

The more psychological question here, however, is not only how such stories travel, but why they are *believed*. The first answer is that we believe them because we are motivated to believe them—they confirm the beliefs that we already hold about our enemies.[47] As noted above, categories help us to understand the world. But they also tend to make the content within them seem more homogenous. When we have an image of a group, if we hear more information about that group, we will tend to select from that information and remember those aspects that are consistent with what we already believe. Imagine that an Azerbaijani hears about activities of Armenians during the war over Nagorno-Karabakh, including activities that are consistent with the devalued image of Armenians (for example, brutality during war) and activities that are inconsistent with that image (for example, bravery and honor in battle). The research discussed here would suggest that the information that person will remember will be the information that is consistent with his or her image of the enemy, while the rest will be less attended to. And when the person repeats what he or she has heard, the information that will be most salient (Allport's "sharpening") will be those aspects that are most illustrative of the person's image of Armenians.

So from a purely cognitive viewpoint, here is why atrocity stories circulate: Once we have a consciousness of ourselves as part of a group, we tend both to homogenize and to devalue the other, rival group. Once we have a devalued image of that group, we will be prone to believe negative stories that we hear about them, or to select the most negative elements from stories that we hear. Then when we repeat the stories, we will repeat those most negative elements, since they will be most salient to us.

The second reason we believe rumors and atrocity stories, according to those who study rumor, is that people want to make sense of their surroundings, and telling such stories helps us to do so. Situations that are ambiguous, where people do not really know what is going on, tend to produce rumors. We as humans have a desire to simplify our surroundings and make our situation comprehensible, to create what Allport and Postman term "effort after meaning" (p. 5). They base this suggestion on the research tradition in psychology known as the Gestalt approach, which focuses on the human tendency to want to bring closure, coherence, and simplicity to the perceptions we have around us. If we see a figure that looks like a triangle yet is missing one point, we still recognize it as a triangle because our minds simply fill in the missing information. In cognitive terms, we have a drive to make sense of information. In emotional terms, too, we want to make sense of our situation. If we are fighting in a war, we want to know why. If we have a *reason* for fighting, it is much easier for us to continue, to endure the hardships we may be experiencing. On a broader scale, rumors can serve a problem-solving function for a whole society; they help the society come to terms with many of the situations it finds itself in.[48]

Thus, in a situation of nationalist conflict, there is another set of very good reasons for listening to, remembering, and repeating atrocity stories. "Why are we fighting against them?" we might ask ourselves. Then we answer: "Because they are evil, and brutal; look at what they did in X situation, and Y situation. Given what they have done, there is no way we can trust them. Fighting is the only way to preserve our dignity,"—or "our land," or "our families," or "our resources," or "justice." Atrocity stories fit with our negative images and make nationalist conflict, and our willing or unwilling participation in it, comprehensible.

In sum, many of the thinking processes we use every day facilitate our entering into conflict. We divide ourselves up into groups. Once we do so, we tend to believe the best about our own group and the worst about others. We then assimilate new information into those images, and the stage is set for conflict.

Riots and Mob Violence

Riots are another form of nationalist conflict, and they also often occur in familiar patterns. As I noted earlier, a second group of Tamils, known as the "Indian" or "Estate" Tamils, lives in the tea-growing highlands of southern Sri Lanka. Until recently the Estate Tamils had not been involved in the conflict in Sri Lanka; the LTTE and other rebel groups were composed of Tamils from the north. However, on October 25, 2000, Sinhalese villagers in this area overran a government-run rehabilitation camp for LTTE soldiers in a town called Bandarawela. They massacred 26 of the inmates there, including one who was from an Estate Tamil village, by beating them with sticks and stabbing them with knives.[49] In response, Tamils held demonstrations and, in some cases, rioted, in a number of highland villages including a Tamil-majority village called Talawakele.[50]

I visited Talawakele not long after the riots and was shown the burned-out shops, houses, and cars that the Tamil rioters had attacked. The villagers reported that the people who burned their houses were Tamils who the villagers knew from the local area, nearly all of them young men. They described in detail the focus and determination of the rioters, who picked out only Sinhalese houses and shops to destroy. The villagers also accused the LTTE and "outsiders" of instigating the riots and aggravating relations between the local peoples, and this accusation was echoed by other observers I talked to in the area. Many of those villagers were now staying in the local Buddhist temple under the care and protection of the local monk, and several of them said they had nowhere else they could go, now that their homes and their livelihoods were gone.

The massacre at Bandarawela and the subsequent riots followed a pattern that, unfortunately, has been seen in Sri Lanka before. On July 24, 1983, LTTE cadres killed 13 Sri Lankan soldiers in the Tamil-dominated Jaffna district of northern Sri Lanka. The soldiers were Sinhalese, as is nearly all of Sri Lanka's army. After the Sri Lankan army brought the bodies back to the Sri Lankan capital, Colombo, and displayed them in the central cemetery, riots broke out. For three days Sinhalese mobs sought out Tamil residents and burned and looted their houses and workplaces, killing at least 362 in Colombo and more in other towns.[51] It is alleged that government security forces allowed the riots to take place and perhaps even encouraged them.[52]

And the riots in the industrial Azerbaijani city of Sumgait in February 1988 followed a similar pattern. After reports that two Azerbaijanis had been killed near Nagorno-Karabakh, rioters rampaged through the Armenian section of Sumgait. The riots continued from February 27 through February 29, and it was reported that the local Azerbaijani authorities did little to stop them. The riots were violent and brutal. Azerbaijanis are reported to have burned people alive, attacked children and old people, and committed rapes and other atrocities. At the end of the riots, the official death toll was 26 Armenians, with other estimates ranging much higher.[53]

In all of these riots, for example, the chain of events seems fairly clear: One group is alleged to have killed members of another group. In retaliation, people whose ingroup members were killed then take revenge, not on those in the outgroup who actually did the killing, but on other members of the group. It is possible that these riots were spontaneous mob uprisings; however, there have been accusations in all of these riots that prior planning took place. In the Colombo riots, for example, allegations have been made that the rioters had voter lists and addresses that could tell them where specific Tamils lived, and that they had government-owned trucks, buses, and trains to transport them.[54] If true, these details would suggest that there was not only organization in the riots, but prior planning.[55] Similarly, in Sumgait, allegations have been made that the rioters had lists that told them where Armenians lived, so they could be easily found.[56] Some have suggested that the Soviet government was behind these riots, either by hiring Armenian thugs to spark the riots (as I was told in Azerbaijan) or even by taking incarcerated Azerbaijani criminals out of a prison and using the KGB to bus them to Sumgait.[57]

Whether the riots were planned or were spontaneous outbreaks of violence, however, one question that arises is why people act as brutally as they do. Whereas many of the stories of atrocities that I reported earlier have not been verified, a glance at almost any newspaper can tell us that people often act with extreme brutality toward one another, far beyond what might be necessary to achieve some tangible goal. In the recent conflict in Bosnia, women were systematically brutalized and raped during episodes of "ethnic cleansing." Torture and beatings in detention are common phenomena during conflicts. Thus any explanation of nationalist conflict will have to explain these extreme forms of violence along with other forms that occur. The approaches I have examined in this chapter do not yet do so.

Conclusions

When people categorize themselves into groups, and particularly into national groups, predictable phenomena arise. These phenomena—such as ingroup favoritism, outgroup devaluation, spreading of rumors, and acting brutally toward one another—have been observed over and over again. The question at this point is, why? Why are we so predictable in our intergroup interactions? Psychology has provided some explanations for this kind of behavior, and the next chapter will examine and evaluate them.

Chapter 2

THE EXPLANATIONS SO FAR

Psychological research and thinking have come up with a number of potential theories to explain nationalism and other types of group conflict. Some explanations say that conflict comes primarily from the actions of a small number of extremists, and those are the ones we need to focus on. Others would say that group aggression is a natural consequence of competition over resources, and nationalism is just one variety of that. Others highlight our tendency to conform to social norms or our biological tendency toward aggression. And yet others would say that group conflict is a way of dealing with anxiety.

Each of these explanations offers important clues, but each of them also has significant limitations. Some emphasize the individual and ignore the social context, whereas others emphasize the social context and ignore the individual. In this chapter I will examine these various approaches, focus on their most important elements, and find a common element that works at both the individual and the social level and explains the tenacity and the vehemence of nationalist conflict.

Agitators, Hooligans, and Bigots?

One of the most vivid features of nationalism is riots and other mob violence, as I described in the last chapter. When riots and pogroms occur, explanations often focus on a few individuals who are said to have stirred up or goaded the rioters into acting. The day after the Tamil detainees were killed in Bandarawela, for example, the president of Sri Lanka identified "provocation from external forces" as the cause of the riot.[1] Some of the villagers I spoke with made the same accusation. Similarly, some have claimed that although the riots in Colombo in 1983 started with the reactions of the dead soldiers' relatives, others, such as smugglers, criminals, some Sinhala politicians, and militant Buddhist monks, fanned the violence for their own reasons.[2] Similar accusations have been made about the instigators of the Sumgait riots—that they were brought in from outside Sumgait in order to cause trouble.[3] In a different context, authorities in England have often accused small numbers of "hooligans" or "yobs" as being at the root of soccer violence there.[4]

Could it be that nationalist violence is primarily the work of a few extremists? Are there personality qualities that characterize "typical" nationalists? To answer this question, we first have to recognize that in some situations people will participate in violence because they will gain something tangible from it. In a riot, for example, individuals can benefit personally from looting. (In an ironic twist, the rioters in Talawakele had looted a Sinhalese shop and stolen brand new television sets and videocassette recorders. However, one of the television sets, still in its new box, fell out of the truck that the looters were using. The box was then found and eventually given to the Buddhist monk in the town who was housing refugees from the riots!) Similarly, individuals can profit from arms sales or smuggling if they incite others to fight in a secessionist war. Politicians can remain in power if they can convince their people that they are fighting in a just war. So there can be very material reasons for engaging in conflict.

And yet not all people who engage in violence immediately profit from it. In Sumgait, violence against Armenians seemed to be the point of the riots, rather than a byproduct of them. Is there evidence that some people are psychologically more predisposed than others to hooliganism, extremism, and violence?

Our everyday experience would suggest that there *are* some people who have more extreme attitudes and are more prejudiced, more prone to violence than others. And in fact there is a long line of research that has investigated this idea. The most famous of these approaches was that of T. W. Adorno and his colleagues, which was presented in a book titled *The Authoritarian Personality*.[5] The authors conducted an extensive research program, involving broad surveys as well as intensive psychological investigations of a smaller number of individuals. This research began around the time of World War II, in response to the threat of fascism in Europe. Many wondered why fascism appealed to people. One answer that emerged from this research is that there are some individuals whose very personality structure makes them prone to see the world as a dangerous place, in which people have to fight for themselves or, failing that, must find a protector.[6] Such a person would feel most comfortable in a society with strict hierarchies, so the person could know where he or she stands. People with an "authoritarian" or "prejudiced" personality, as this character type was called, were said to be distinguished by feeling ambivalence toward parents, being highly moralistic, tending to see the world in black and white, needing definiteness, seeing the causes of events as outside of his or her control, believing in strong social order, and needing hierarchy and authority.[7] Ethnocentrism and prejudice were seen to pervade such a person's entire personality.

This research lost favor after a number of years, but it has not died out entirely. More recent studies have continued to affirm the existence of an "authoritarian personality," and more specifically a *right-wing* authoritarian personality, in which submission to authority, aggression that is sanctioned by authority, and a need for order and convention are primary.[8] (In this case, the "right-wing" label refers to attitudes toward authority rather than specific political beliefs.) Another recent book has vividly and richly examined the ideas and thinking processes of "the racist mind," through interviews with white supremacists here in the United States.[9] And there may be a particular constellation of personality qualities in those who are likely to riot at sporting events.[10]

What has this research tradition helped us understand about nationalism? It is clear that there are individual differences in the degree to which people can tolerate ambiguity, how strongly and negatively they feel about other groups, and to what degree they think that hierarchical structures are important for society. So there are some people who, by the nature of their habitual ways of thinking and feeling, are more likely to be active in a nationalist cause, and others who are less likely. And certainly that fits with everyday experience. Some people emerge as leaders in nationalist struggles, while others support the movements either fully or partly. We all know some people with very strong ideas, feelings, and opinions about current issues, and others who tend to be less strong in this regard. And even in an ethnic riot, one of the most extreme forms of violence, not everyone responds exactly the same way. Indeed, there are many stories of Sinhalese shielding their Tamil neighbors from harm in the anti-Tamil riots in Colombo in 1983,[11] and I heard the same from the Sinhalese villagers in Talawakele about the riots against them in 2000.

And yet this focus on individuals does not explain everything. People act differently in different situations. The same villagers that I drove past in

Talawakele had rioted against their neighbors two weeks earlier, but they were not rioting the day I was there, and they had not rioted before the massacre at the Bandarawela camp. In general, nationalist violence tends to happen in brief outbreaks at times of high tension, and then fades away for a while. The explanation that "hooligans" are behind nationalist riots must be missing something, because where are those hooligans in between times?

There are also other difficulties. "Personality" is difficult to measure, since it can only be *inferred* from people's behavior or from their responses to questions. And even when we develop methods to measure personality and believe we have a good description of what "personality" is, there is no assurance that it is consistent; will one's attitudes toward authority, for example, be the same in a week or a year? If not, can we really say that there is a "personality" that persists over time and over different situations? Many psychologists have argued that focusing on the personality qualities of individuals ignores the extreme power that the situation can and does exert on behavior.[12] And even if it may be true in some cases that there are "agitators" who stir up ethnic or nationalist hostility for their own reasons, the fact remains that many of us *respond* to such agitation. There must be other dynamics underlying nationalist violence, particularly given its episodic character.

Cultural and Social Conditions

Might there be particular cultural and social conditions that predispose societies, and the individuals in them, to violence? In a comparison of the Holocaust, the genocide of the Armenians in Turkey in 1915, the mass killings in Cambodia between 1975 and 1979, and the "disappearances" of thousands of people in Argentina beginning in 1976, Ervin Staub asserts that "difficult life conditions" are among the circumstances that can lead a society to genocide.[13] Such conditions would include rapid social change, homelessness, unemployment, and political conflict, all of which lead people to feel uncertain about the future and to feel disconnected from each other. Scapegoating a minority or a national group other than their own helps to provide people with a sense of meaning—instead of wondering why they feel lost or anxious, people can simply blame that group for their problems, and suddenly the world seems more comprehensible. Staub also notes that as societies tolerate and condone violence, it becomes a way of life, and new generations learn the same techniques of blaming others, and the more the others are blamed, the more it seems that they deserve the condemnation they are getting.[14]

Staub thus adds a temporal dimension to his explanation of genocidal violence: In times of high social change, we might expect more violence; and in times of relative stability, we would expect less. This suggestion certainly accords with the experience of Armenia and Azerbaijan over Nagorno-Karabakh. There was a great deal of conflict between Armenians and Azerbaijanis when the Russian Empire was disintegrating between 1905 and 1917,[15] and then comparatively little conflict during the Soviet period, from the early 1920s to 1988. Then, when the Soviet Union began to disintegrate, conflict between the two groups flared up again, including riots against Armenians in Sumgait and Baku, an apparent massacre of Azerbaijanis in the town of Khojaly, and the full-scale war over Nagorno-Karabakh. The conflict has been most intense during periods of major social and economic change in the region.

Staub also suggests that there are cultural qualities that may predispose a society to mass violence, including a sense among the majority that they are deserving of success, combined with an underlying insecurity; a history of devaluing a subgroup; obedience to authority as a major cultural value; and a monolithic (as opposed to a pluralistic) political culture. In Sri Lanka, Sinhalese nationalists have both a sense of entitlement (Sri Lanka is the historical home of Theravada Buddhism, and thus Sri Lanka should be Buddhist) and a sense of insecurity (there are 50 million Tamils in Southern India, and so the Sinhalese could be overwhelmed by them).[16] In the last half century at least, and perhaps also earlier, the Sinhalese majority has devalued the Tamil minority, particularly in power-sharing in the post-independence political arrangements. Sri Lanka as a society has also tolerated a great deal of violence, not only in the conflict between Tamil separatists and the government, but between the government and political groups—particularly the Janatha Vimukthi Peramuna (JVP), a militant Sinhalese youth organization that engaged in violent confrontations with the government in 1971 and from 1987 to 1990. The JVP assassinated politicians, government officials, and members of the armed forces, and the government responded by terrorizing the civilian population through abductions and executions of suspected JVP sympathizers, including leaving the tortured bodies of executed people on piles of burning tires along roadsides.[17] Sri Lanka's government has made a variety of attempts to be pluralistic rather than monolithic, but the political pressures, particularly from Sinhalese nationalists, have at times made that very difficult.[18]

So Staub's analysis helps us understand that there are large social and cultural factors that might make violence more likely. But questions still remain. Nationalist violence is episodic not only in that it happens in some historical periods and not in others, but also in that people engage in conflict only at particular moments, in particular places, rather than all the time. Why might a riot happen in one particular city and not another? To understand the specific nature of such conflict, we would have to look more closely at the immediate situation surrounding it.

Conflict Over Resources

It could be that the reason people engage in conflict is that they are simply competing over resources. Wouldn't it make sense that, if someone else has what we want, and especially what we feel we deserve, we would try to take it from them? And isn't it likely that we would become angry at them in the process? Realistic Group Conflict Theory[19] is a prominent psychological approach to understanding group hostility that focuses on competition over resources as the operative dynamic underlying intergroup conflict.[20] The theory itself was developed in controlled situations rather than through studying real-world conflicts.

For example, in the most famous series of studies, the "Robbers Cave" Experiment, researchers gathered a number of boys from Oklahoma and randomly divided them into two groups. The boys were taken to a summer camp, where the two groups engaged (separately, each unaware of the other group's existence) in normal summer camp activities. Over the first week, the groups developed group identities (the Rattlers and the Eagles) and social structures. After a week, the researchers brought the groups together for a series of competitions. Sure enough, hostility and prejudice developed quickly between the two groups. After the Eagles lost a game, they found a Rattlers' flag and burned it. Then the next day, the Rattlers stole the Eagles' flag when the Eagles arrived at the playing field. Even more interesting is that when the researchers asked the boys to rate their impressions of the other group, a large proportion of the boys in each group rated all of the other group's members as having undesirable personalities.[21] This kind of outgroup devaluation is exactly what was described in the previous chapter, and it seems to have been produced by the situation in which the boys found themselves—intergroup competition.

Obviously, there is a similarity between these studies and the experiences of my students in the group work of the Nationalism course. The hostility that the Gatekeepers engendered among the other groups when they all competed over presentation times was palpable. And it did not stop as the semester went on. The Gatekeepers controlled the door, and they used that resource to frustrate and anger the other groups by denying them access to it. The Smooth Operators had control of the telephone in the room, and competition and hostility developed over its use, too. Indeed, many studies confirm that competition can produce hostility between groups.[22] Could it be that competition over resources is the reason that people get into conflict and engage in it so violently?

To know whether or not this argument makes sense, we have to examine the evidence carefully. First, as in much of psychological research, the studies in which these ideas were developed were deliberately conducted outside of a real-world context. The researchers typically took people who did not know each other and had no shared history, put them into groups, and manipulated the resources available, as I did in my class. Using controlled situations like this prevents potentially confounding variables from interfering in the process; if hostility between the groups erupted, the researchers could confidently conclude that it was the social situation that caused the hostility, rather than the individuals involved. This is good practice in psychological research. However, it raises many issues about whether or not these results really are generalizable to the real world of nationalist conflicts. In real-life conflicts, the groups involved nearly always have some kind of history together, and competition over resources is nearly always intertwined with many other issues, such as historical experiences and religious differences. Can we really ascribe the cause of conflict to resource competition, when so many other factors are present at the same time? Put another way, competition over resources might be enough to cause nationalist hostility. But does there *have* to be such competition to produce hostility?

In the conflicts we are examining here, resource issues are common. Nagorno-Karabakh is a forested and fertile area with mineral resources lying beneath the soil, whereas much of the land around it in Armenia and Azerbaijan is arid. For that reason, Nagorno-Karabakh is economically valuable. In Sri Lanka, Tamils were overrepresented (in terms of their proportion in the population) in public service jobs under the British; and so, after independence, the Sri Lankan government established laws that would promote the Sinhalese in employment, such as making the minimum scores for university entrance lower for Sinhalese than they were for Tamils.[23] Jobs are a very clear economic resource. In addition, the proposed state of Tamil Eelam would occupy much of the coastline of Sri Lanka, which would have large implications for shipping, fishing, and tourism. These conflicts obviously have important resource issues. In fact, it would be difficult to find a conflict that does not involve some kind of resource, be it natural resources, strategic location, or access to jobs, goods, and services.

Hence we can accept that competition over resources can play an important role in developing conflict. However, resources do not explain everything. I met former soldiers who were native to Yerevan yet who fought in Nagorno-Karabakh. Other soldiers came from as far away as California.[24] Those who came to fight from Yerevan or from abroad had no immediate stake in the resources that Nagorno-Karabakh might provide for those who lived there, nor were they directly threatened by the Azerbaijanis. Nonetheless, they risked their lives and fought in the conflict. Similarly, much of the funding for the LTTE comes from Sri Lankan Tamils who currently live outside of Sri Lanka.[25] They have no immediate economic stake in whether or not Tamil Eelam becomes a reality. And finally, in the Psychology of Nationalism course, ingroup hostility developed even when the "resources" involved were "resource chips" (or "points") that I allotted to each group after each session. These chips were worthless for anything but keeping score between the groups. So there must be other issues that drive conflict beyond simply the realistic resources involved.

Mob Rule?

Other psychological thinking suggests that simply being put into a group may be enough to produce conflict—that when we get into a group we tend to go along with the crowd and simply do whatever we want, and that what we want is typically to be aggressive, hostile, and sexual. This idea has a long history in psychological thinking. Gustave LeBon, in the late 1800s, was one of the first to promote the idea that when people get into a group, the group somehow takes them over, and their individual personalities disappear into a common "group mind." The intellectual level of that mind, he argued, is much lower than the level of the individuals who make it up. He described the phenomenon by saying:

> By the mere fact that he forms part of an organized crowd, a man descends several rungs in the ladder of civilization. Isolated, he may be a cultivated individual; in a crowd, he is a barbarian—that is, a creature acting by instinct.[26]

Sigmund Freud later built upon LeBon's ideas, highlighting that mobs tend to be impulsive, irritable, suggestible, and irrational, and that individuals in group situations tend to experience heightened emotion and lowered intellectual functioning.[27] Obviously, on the surface, the riot stories I have related seem to bear out this description. People do not ordinarily burn houses and loot buildings in everyday life, but they do in riots. We could explain this observation simply by saying that inhibitions against antisocial activity deteriorate in a group situation. If being in a group lowers our inhibitions or our ability to control our impulses, then we would participate in riots as a way to gratify desires for excitement or for obtaining goods that we otherwise would have to buy.[28]

So it is possible that being in a group simply takes away our inhibitions. Why would that be? One suggestion is that we lose a sense of our identity, and with it, a lessening of individual responsibility for the acts that we are committing. Psychologists have given this process the name "deindividuation," and many laboratory experiments have suggested that if people are anonymous (for example, if their faces cannot be seen), they will be much more likely to be aggressive toward others.[29] Again, this idea makes intuitive sense; if no one can know our identity (if we were in a mob, for example), then perhaps we would feel less responsibility for our actions. Those actions do not necessarily have to be antisocial, however. Other studies have suggested that prosocial feelings can be expressed in conditions of anonymity, too.[30]

Related to this idea is "diffusion of responsibility," which is the idea that when there are a number of people in a setting, each of them individually feels less responsibility than he or she would if alone. This too has been demonstrated in many research studies.[31] This process might easily make us less likely to refrain when others around us are committing antisocial acts. In addition, conformity may play a role; it is difficult to deviate from what a group around us is doing if we fear that by doing so, we will be less liked or might be ostracized.[32]

These social psychological concepts make intuitive sense. It does seem that wearing a uniform or being a seemingly anonymous member of a crowd might lead us to believe that we are not responsible for our individual actions; after all, everyone is doing it, and who is going to know? Similarly, we have probably all felt the desire to conform to social norms at some time in our lives. However, much of the research that supports these ideas suffers from the problems of all laboratory research. The conditions of laboratory experiments are artificial; the external conditions are highly controlled so that the researchers can be sure what factors caused what. But can such research generalize to a real-life situation of nationalist conflict, in which the history between the groups, political or economic disparities, or recent or past atrocities may play central roles? The particular conditions that make laboratory research good—especially the ability to control variables—make the results of experiments less likely to be generalizable to complex real-world situations.

In particular, we need to ask one question: If deindividuation and diffusion of responsibility explain group violence, then shouldn't such violence be more indiscriminate? If the rioters in Sumgait were deindividuated and did not feel responsibility for their actions, why did they not attack *everyone?* Why did they target only Armenians? Similarly, why did the Colombo rioters target only Tamils, and in particular, why did they specifically destroy Tamil businesses? One answer to these questions flows from the ingroup-outgroup concepts discussed in chapter 1. Nationalist riots or other violent intergroup behavior comes in a particular context—the context of an intergroup situation in which each group has a learned set of cognitive and emotional responses to the other group. In a sense, the members of each group in a nationalist situation must have a concept of who is the ingroup and who is the outgroup, and they must have ways of distinguishing between them. And once they know who the members of the outgroup are, then all outgroup members seem the same. The Azerbaijanis in Sumgait attacked Armenians. These Armenians may have lived in Sumgait for many years and might have been as fluent in Russian as in Armenian. Yet the Azerbaijanis apparently considered them similar enough to those who caused the trouble in Nagorno-Karabakh to direct violence against them. So ingroup-outgroup thinking, combined with deindividuation and diffusion of responsibility, might account for episodes of nationalist or ethnic violence.

But there is another set of possible answers. Might nationalist violence be not simply spontaneous outbreaks of mob hostility, but instead organized attempts to brutalize a specific group of people? If so, then what kinds of psychological dynamics would underlie the organizing and carrying out of such actions?

Organization and Obedience

As I noted earlier, many accusations have surfaced that the behavior of the rioters in Talawakele, Colombo, and Sumgait was not random. The rioters were said to have voting lists or other ways of determining where Armenians (in Sumgait) and Tamils (in Colombo) lived. In Talawakele, the villagers told me that the mobs seem to be led by individuals who searched out specifically Sinhalese businesses and homes.

If this is true, then we need to examine the *organized* aspects of rioting and not just its disinhibited aspects. Herbert Kelman is one long-time researcher of nationalist and ethnic conflict who has described a number of ways in which organization might exacerbate violence and even genocide. He describes three factors—authorization, routinization, and dehumanization—that characterize what happens in riots and other examples of organized mass violence.[33]

The first of these processes is authorization. If a person believes that his or her activities have been given sanction by a higher authority, then he or she is more likely to commit aggressive acts, because the normal moral strictures against such acts are taken away. Whether or not a particular act was "authorized" was a large part of the investigation into the My Lai massacre in Vietnam, when a group of American soldiers killed more than 128 unarmed inhabitants of a Vietnamese village. The soldiers claimed that they were ordered to carry out the killings, and an officer, Lieutenant William Calley, eventually stood trial for 102 of them (he was convicted of 22).[34] Kelman and his colleague Lee Hamilton argue that although hatred and rage seemed to play a part in these killings, as in other sanctioned massacres, it is the following of orders by the soldiers, rather than hatred, that is the real instigator of such violence.[35]

Routinization and dehumanization are two other social processes that facilitate mass violence. Routinization is making killing into a job, so that it is not necessary to make individual decisions of what to do each time. Dehumanization is the process of treating the "others" as though they are not real people, by giving them numbers, calling them names ("terrorists" or "gooks"), or by referring to them literally as animals. Dehumanization is an extension of outgroup devaluation, which, as we have seen, is very common in conflict situations. And again, seeing everyone in the outgroup as the same also plays into this process; if one outgroup member is guilty of some crime, then all may seem to be equally guilty.

It is easy to see how these processes might operate in the Nagorno-Karabakh and Sri Lankan conflicts. If in fact there were LTTE infiltrators directing the riots in the hill country in Sri Lanka in 2000, as the villagers alleged, or if the (predominantly Sinhalese) security forces stood by in 1983 and watched the riots in Colombo, as has been widely reported,[36] or even if there were left-wing or Communist agitators directing the riots in 1983, as the Sri Lankan government claimed, then the rioters themselves may have felt more free to carry out their violence since they believed it was authorized. In quasi-military or military operations, these processes are even more likely to take place. Such could have been the process at Khojaly, for example, a town in Azerbaijan where, it is alleged, Armenian troops massacred hundreds of Azerbaijanis, including women and children, on February 25 and 26, 1992.[37] When an authority sanctions the use of force, atrocities and violence become more likely.

The Power of Roles

One way of implicitly sanctioning behavior is to put someone into a social role. It turns out that if we are given a social role and an expectation that we should carry out that role, we will do so. One of the most often cited demonstrations of this process was the "Stanford Prison Experiment," carried out by Philip Zimbardo and his associates at Stanford University.[38] In that study, researchers divided a group of male college students into two groups and told them that they would be either prisoners or guards in a mock prison set up in the basement of the Psychology Department's building. The researchers arranged with the local police to "arrest" those students who were to be the prisoners, who were then dressed in hospital gowns, given stockings to wear over their hair, and referred to only by their prison numbers. The "guards" were given uniforms and dark glasses and told that their job was to keep order in the prison.

The main result of this demonstration was that within days of beginning the study, the students who were the prisoners began to show the behavior characteristics of real prisoners, including passivity, dependency, and helplessness. The guards, in contrast, became more authoritarian in their approach to the prisoners, and even, in some cases, sadistic. The study had to be called off after only one week because the situation became potentially harmful to the psychological well-being of the "inmates."

The point of this study is that, as was the case with the Robbers Cave experiment, people divided by the random flip of a coin into different groups could be led to behave in ways that are very different from their usual behavior. Role expectations, diffusion of responsibility, a desire not to stand out from others—all of these are social forces that can combine to push us into aggressive behavior. Perhaps the most important conclusion of this social-psychological research is the exact opposite of that on the authoritarian personality. This research suggests that any of us, if put into the right situation, might well take part in nationalist (or other) violence, even without any particular predisposing family history or personality traits. Though certainly there are individual differences in our predisposition to engage in conflict, the situation is very powerful; if we had been there, we too might have engaged in the violence in Nazi Germany, in

Bosnia, in Nagorno-Karabakh, or in Sri Lanka. These are humbling conclusions that many social psychologists hope will lead us to pay more attention to the way we structure our societies.

Thus social-psychological explanations shed light on the power of the immediate situation and provide some explanations for why individuals—and not only extremists—take part in nationalist violence. However, there are issues that the social-psychological explanations do not explain as well. For example, we can understand how people might get caught up in the social interactions of the moment. If one person harms another, an angry and defensive reaction would be expected. But where does the *rage* come from? Why do people go to such lengths to brutalize one another—mutilating corpses, cutting off ears or genitals, laying waste to property? Why is sexual violence such a common atrocity in wars and nationalist conflicts? Why do people commit violent acts that seem vastly out of proportion to any provocation? The social-psychological research begins to explain under what *conditions* conflict might occur. But we need some way of beginning to understand the more primitive emotional aspects of conflict, and how they tie in to the nationalist identity that is so often part of such conflicts.

Psychodynamic Explanations for Violence and Rage

Psychodynamic psychology is the one psychological approach that offers some suggestions as to why conflict can be characterized by such brutality and viciousness. Freud himself did not really make many forays into discussing nationalism, aside from commenting on the tendency of people to express animosity toward people who live nearby and who are like them, which he called "the narcissism of minor differences."[39] In general, Freud saw aggression as a primitive instinct that needed to be satisfied. Instincts, in Freud's view, have a power of their own; if there are societal strictures against expressing them (as there are for sexual and aggressive instincts in particular), then they will seek expression somehow, either directly or in disguised form. One way to satisfy this need for release of aggressive impulses is to turn them outward onto scapegoats or enemies.

Later theorists have taken this conception of aggression, elaborated upon it, and applied it to an understanding of ethnic and nationalist conflict. The story of nationalism, from this point of view, might go this way: Each one of us, by virtue of being human, experiences very primitive emotions in early life. Primary among these emotions are love and aggression. When we are one or two or three years old, when we feel these emotions, we feel them viscerally, and they are very powerful. However, we do not have the emotional and cognitive complexity to be able to integrate these various aspects of ourselves—to understand that our anger, our shame, our love, and all our other feelings are a part of us. Instead, we tend to "split" the world into "good" and "bad." We also tend to take those aspects of ourselves that we have not integrated and experience them as being outside ourselves, just as a child playing with stuffed animals might attribute her emotions to those animals. (In psychoanalytic terms, this is known as "externalization.") As we grow older, we begin to be able to integrate all of those feelings into our own self-image. At the same time, though, we begin to learn that expressing primitive impulses (especially sexual and aggressive ones) is discouraged by society, and so we learn to be ashamed of those impulses. That shame can give rise to another defense mechanism, called "projection." This is where we unconsciously take those aspects of ourselves that we do not like (typically the sexual and aggressive impulses) and attribute them to others. This works especially well when we have traditional enemies, who serve as our habitual targets for those projections. In addition, during times of stress, we tend to regress back to that pattern of splitting the world into "good" and "bad," so that we see our enemies not just as evil, immoral, lustful, and hateful, but being so in truly black-and-white terms. Thus the negative images we have of our enemies are fueled not only by whatever reality there is in our perceptions of them, but by the emotional power of our own unwanted aspects of ourselves. We can justifiably condemn these "enemies" because they embody all of the things that we hate the most in ourselves. And killing them would be an unconscious attempt to rid ourselves of those hateful qualities forever.[40]

The first virtue of this approach is that it begins to explain the vehemence of ethnic and nationalist conflict. Remember that in the psychodynamic approach, emotions are understood to be quite primitive. The anger that we feel about the unwanted aspects of ourselves is not simple dislike or disdain; it is *rage*. And thus when we see the absolute worst about ourselves in our enemies, we do not simply dislike them—we want to *exterminate* them, to get rid of those qualities that (unconsciously) we want to exterminate in ourselves. Thus the mutilation of bodies, the indiscriminate killing of noncombatants, the mass rape and other sexual violence can be seen as psychologically motivated—as expressions of primitive rage directed away from the self.

The second useful aspect of this approach is that it begins to explain the *tenacity* of conflict. The psychoanalyst Vamik Volkan has written a book titled *The Need to Have Enemies and Allies*,[41] in which he uses this approach to argue that having enemies serves a *purpose* for us. In providing an appropriate "receptacle" for our unwanted projections, the nationalist enemy helps keep us psychologically stable. Thus we can see why we might be reluctant to give up enemies and might perhaps even search for new enemies if our old ones are defeated. And finally, there is a developmental hierarchy implicit in this theory. The more that people have integrated their aggressive feelings into their personalities, the less likely they would be to project them onto other people. This is also a suggestion made by the research on the "authoritarian personality" (since both are derived from psychodynamic theory), and it begins to explain the observed range of individual differences in how people engage in nationalist conflict. The social-psychological approaches described above, since they focus on situations that affect everyone equally, are not as well equipped to explain those differences.

Thus this approach begins to fill in some of the gaps in our understanding of nationalism, and aspects of it will be very useful in the unified approach that I will propose. However, it also has some disadvantages. First, this approach has the difficulty of using concepts that are derived from the study of individuals (defense mechanisms like externalization or projection) to describe large groups. As social psychology would point out, groups are not simply aggregations of individuals; there are processes (such as conformity and the acting out of social roles) that come into being only in social contexts. Second, much of the information used by theorists in this tradition is from psychotherapy. Material derived from clinical psychiatric or psychological practice, however vivid, may not accurately represent the ways that all people function, given the specific qualities of that population. Third, like most psychological theories, this approach tends to be acontextual—it claims to apply to anyone, anywhere. And yet the historical experiences of groups in the world are very different from each other, and there needs to be some clear link between the experiences of the individual and those of the group.[42] And finally, this approach does not provide an obvious way to account for the dynamic nature of nationalist conflict. How could people who live next door to each other live peacefully one day and then riot against each other the next? If the argument centers around character structure, which it largely does, then it is hard to see how the same individuals could act so differently toward the same people at different times.

Overall, the psychodynamic approach has some strong points. It begins to explain the vehemence and the tenacity of conflict, and opens a window onto the emotional aspects of nationalism, which the social approaches do not do well. However, it does not account for the dynamic and shifting nature of nationalist conflict and of the contexts in which it occurs.

Biological Explanations

Finally, there are biological approaches that have tried to explain nationalist conflict. Some have claimed that our evolutionary heritage has saddled us with the tendency to group together along racial or kinship lines. Others note that since men are the ones most often involved in conflict, examining the role of testosterone might provide clues to why we act the way we do. Can a look at the evolutionary and biological contexts of humanity help us understand the way that anger and hatred are involved in nationalist violence?

The first answer might be simply yes—humans do get into nationalist conflicts because we are simply aggressive by nature, as are many other species. Aggression might be an instinct. Just like any other trait, if it increases the chances of survival of the individual or the species, it is *selected for* and will therefore show up more in the next generation. Aggression might be selected for because, for example, animals might need to fight or to kill in competing with other species for food. Those who get the food survive long enough to reproduce.[43] The same argument might also be made for aggression within a species. Aggression would help to balance the distribution of a population over a widely spaced area—if members of a species got so close together that they might deplete the available resources, intraspecific aggression would keep them far enough apart to prevent that. Aggression might also produce the best offspring, because males fight off other males for the best females, and so the genes for strength and intelligence would be propagated. This in turn is good for the species and for the family group, because when a group is surrounded or threatened it is these males who defend it. This general evolutionary approach emphasizes that our nervous systems evolved over millions of years, and that in the vast majority of that time, people lived in small groups without abundant resources; thus competition over scarce resources was a predictable way of life.

There are several problems with this view, however. First, there is disagreement on whether or not intraspecific violence, such as we see in humans, is really present in other areas of the animal kingdom. Some researchers and theorists suggest that violence and war between members of the same species is widely found in the animal kingdom,[44] and others claim that the opposite is true, that war and violence within a species is rare outside of humans.[45] Second, if aggression were "innate," then societies should not differ widely in levels of aggression. However, anthropological research has demonstrated that, in fact, human societies vary tremendously in their aggressiveness.[46]

More importantly, though, this view does not explain why people are violent only in some situations. Obviously, evolution has provided humans with the capacity to be violent. When we act aggressively, a number of brain structures (typically the amygdala and the hypothalamus) are involved, as are a number of neurotransmitters (such as serotonin) and hormones (in particular, androgens such as testosterone).[47] But we all have these brain structures and these neurotransmitters, and thus we all have the capacity to act aggressively and violently. However, not all of us act violently; even those of us who do act violently do so only at some times and not others. Thus the real question for a biological approach is: What kinds of situations evoke the potential in us to *act* in violent ways? An approach that relies on instinct does not help us until it begins to specify the conditions under which we might be violent.

One possibility might be, as suggested above, that we are violent when we are competing over scarce resources, such as food. Unfortunately, that is not necessarily the case. Animals, and people, will fight over resources that are not scarce at all. For example, chimpanzees as well as humans will fight over *surplus* food—when there are more than enough bananas to go around, chimpanzees will fight over them, just as people will fight over gold or other forms of riches even when they already have enough to supply their needs.[48] So there must be other situational cues that evoke violence aside from scarce resources.

One point that comes from this discussion is that there are different kinds of aggression. Aggression that serves to achieve some specific end, like food or territory, might be called "instrumental aggression."[49] Certainly nationalist conflicts can involve instrumental aggression. If an army commander orders an assault on a rebel camp, that is instrumental aggression. Similarly, if a rioter smashes a store window in order to steal a television set, that is instrumental aggression. This kind of aggression is not particularly puzzling, however. Much more difficult to understand is what might be termed "hostile aggression," such as brutalizing villagers before killing them, or torturing captives, or humiliating or degrading members of other groups.[50] Some have argued that this second kind of aggression comes when someone's goals are frustrated.[51] In fact, it may be that in humans, the aggressive response to frustration is much greater when the "thwarting" of someone's attempts to achieve a goal is perceived to be unjust. Justice may be the issue, rather than simply attaining goals. As we will see in chapter 4, concerns of justice play a very large role in nationalist conflict.

If we are attempting to protect resources that we or our kind can use, is nationalism then simply "tribalism"? Another evolutionary argument is that nationalism and nationalist violence might have evolved as part of an attempt to protect one's family, because doing so ensures that our genes are passed into the next generation.[52] This argument makes sense when we are talking about a small group of nomads, perhaps, all of whom are related. It becomes a bit more problematic when we think about larger groups, however. I cannot possibly be related in any substantial way to all Americans. And yet many have gone to war in defense of "all Americans," just as people (mostly men) have gone to war for centuries to protect their own nations. This evolutionary viewpoint raises an interesting idea, which is that we might feel a pull to defend others only if we have somehow identified them as being like us, or part of us. But how might I feel that all Americans are part of me? In some ways, this evolutionary explanation really becomes a question of identity, as I will discuss in the next chapter.

And lastly, it is true that in nearly every society, men are more likely to be violent and aggressive than women, so there may well be some biological component to the predisposition to violence.[53] How might that work? Testosterone is a hormone that is related to aggressive behavior in men and possibly in women. Men have more testosterone circulating in their bodies, so that could be an explanation for why men tend to be more violent.

However, the relationship between physiology and behavior seems more complicated than that; there may be an intervening factor between the hormones and the eventual aggression. Recent research has suggested that *dominance* is such an intervening factor. Dominance simply refers to status—being more important than someone else, being a winner compared to losers. Levels of testosterone fluctuate according to the time of day and many other factors. Interestingly, they also vary depending on the kinds of competitive and status situations that a person is in. Testosterone levels rise in male athletes before a game or match; and afterward, the levels remain high in the winners while they diminish in the losers. These effects are consistent even in situations where physical activity is not an issue, such as in competitors in chess matches and spectators at sporting events.[54] And testosterone may not only *influence* such behavior, it may *respond* to it also. So status and dominance—how people are viewed by others and who is seen to be more important than whom—could be very clearly related to aggressive behavior in humans, perhaps more for men than for women. As we will see later, comparing ourselves with others is a very powerful part of how we evaluate ourselves.

Most biological approaches will not pretend to be able to explain all human aggressive behavior, and much less to explain the particular historical phenomenon of nationalist and ethnic conflict. However, there are a couple of very important points we can take from this discussion. First, we know that if we want to understand nationalist violence, we need to understand the particular kinds of environmental events that trigger violence. Second, violence can come from more than just competition over resources; threat to kin, or at least to those we have *identified* as being related to us or like us, can provoke violence. And third, dominance—or, in simpler terms, how we compare ourselves to others—is potentially very important.

Conclusion

Each of these explanations adds important suggestions for understanding the psychological dimensions of nationalism. Competition over resources can play a strong role in conflict. There are very real individual differences in how extreme individuals' views are and how violently they are expressed. The larger cultural context and the immediate social situation, including whether and how people are being organized and led, can make a situation much more likely to produce violence and bloodshed. The psychodynamic approach highlights the emotional components of nationalism that are so evident in nationalist violence around the world. And there is a biological component to such violence, which could be connected to both identity and dominance. These explanations are reminders that all of us, not just a select few, have the potential to engage in violence.

But each of these approaches has its own assumptions and its own set of premises. While they are all useful, they are very disjointed. The biological approach, for example, focuses on totally different issues than does the social-psychological approach, and it is hard to see how insights from both could be integrated together. The psychodynamic approach and realistic conflict theory are also at odds, because one (the psychodynamic theory) assumes an emotion-driven, irrational kind of group conflict, whereas the other (Realistic Conflict Theory) assumes that people are driven by somewhat rational considerations about attaining needed resources.

And in terms of achieving a full understanding of the psychological dimensions of nationalism, we still have two other significant problems.

First, we are caught between differing levels of analysis. We have seen individual factors and social factors that may influence conflict, but we do not yet have a way to talk about how those individual and social factors relate to each other. Focusing on individuals leaves out the power of the situation, whereas focusing on the situation ignores the contextual factors of particular conflicts that may be very important. Neither of these approaches is sufficient in itself. And second, because of the relatively ahistorical and acontextual nature of psychological research, we do not have an understanding of how the specific cultural and historical context of a particular people might help to shape their experience of conflict, nor do we even have the means of understanding those contexts. Those concepts would be more useful if they were somehow able to take into account the shared history of the groups and the antagonism that seems to have been built up between them.

What we need is a way of addressing these two problems simultaneously, in a way that draws upon the insights of these various psychological approaches in a unified way. We need, in essence, something that unifies all of these various factors. That unifying factor is identity, and it is the subject of the next two chapters.

Chapter 3

IDENTITY—
THE CONSISTENT FEATURE

In the previous chapter I argued that the explanations that psychology has offered so far do not provide an integrated understanding of nationalist violence. We know about some of the cognitive, social, and individual processes that might facilitate nationalist conflict, but we have no real way of understanding how those processes link together. On the one hand, nationalist conflict is inherently individual; any nationalist rally, or riot, or army is made up of individuals who *participate* in it, for their own individual reasons. At the same time, however, nationalist conflict is inherently social; the people who experience nationalism are identifying with a specific group of people, and they are acting on the basis of that identification. So any comprehensive analysis of nationalist conflict needs to take into account both the social and individual dimensions of such a conflict. It also needs to deal with the particular qualities of national identity, since national identity—out of the many group identities that each of us potentially has—seems to command such passionate loyalty and action in the world.

In this chapter I will propose a single unit of analysis that will provide a window into both the social and individual aspects of nationalism, and allow for a coherent psychological explanation of nationalist conflict. That unit of analysis is identity.

Why Identity?

If we define identity simply as our sense of who we are, then we can see that identity is central to all the various psychological explanations for nationalist conflict reviewed so far. If someone is attempting to take away resources that I need, then I might feel a threat to my own continued existence, which is my identity. If I am in a riot and do not feel responsibility for my own actions, then I am "deindividuated"—I have somehow "lost" my identity. If unacknowledged impulses and drives endanger my sense of who I am or who I "ought" to be, then, similarly, my identity is threatened. And if I attempt to assert my dominance over others, I am acting to protect the status of my identity. The sense of who we are and who we are not runs through all of the psychological approaches to nationalism.

And indeed, we do not have to look far before we find all kinds of identity concerns in the conflicts we have studied. Each begins with a distinction between "us" and "them"—who is a Tamil and who is Sinhalese, who is Armenian and who is Azerbaijani, who is a Gatekeeper and who is a Smooth Operator. And we are very quick to notice that distinction. When the students came in to my Psychology of Nationalism course on that very first day of group work and found their seats arranged in groups, they immediately began commenting on the differences between their groups and the others. The ones in the smallest group (Three Girls and a Guy) expressed concerns about how outnumbered they were, while the largest group, the Gatekeepers, exulted in their "majority" status even before all of the students had arrived in the room. The consciousness of "us" and "them" was evident even before any group interactions had occurred.

In the actual conflicts we have examined, identity obviously matters. At the most basic level, identity mattered in the Sumgait and Colombo riots because it determined whether or not a person was a target. That was the purpose of the lists that the rioters allegedly carried with them in both cases. At a more general level, though, identity runs through the public rhetoric of those involved. For example, consider this opening passage from an Armenian government publication called "Armenia: An Emerging Democracy":

> The history of Armenia actually begins some 2,700 years ago . . . From 95 to 55 B.C.E., Tigranes the Great united the Armenian lands and developed Armenia into a strong empire whose land stretched from the Caspian Sea to the Black Sea and Southward to the Mediterranean. . . . Over the years, although repeatedly invaded, conquered, and ruled by others, the Armenian nation preserved its national and cultural identity. In 301 A.D., Armenia became the first nation to adopt Christianity as its state religion and defiantly retained its autonomous Armenian Apostolic church despite being conquered by several non-Christian invaders.[1]

This passage emphasizes that Armenians have preserved their national identity, over repeated threats, for many years. Protecting that identity, defining its boundaries, is clearly a central task. In addition, the passage suggests that Armenia is more than just the territory of the current Republic of Armenia; Armenia is a concept that stretches across time and extends far beyond today's borders. A national group's identity is not only its image of who it is now, but also who it has been in the past, and who its people hope it will be in the future. That identity might include mythological beginnings or some kind of destiny toward which the nation is perceived to be marching.

And finally, some of the major issues in the conflicts are linked directly to identity because they explicitly threaten it. A major example is the bombing of the Temple of the Tooth in Kandy, as I described earlier. There are a number of ways in which Sinhalese people might have perceived this attack as a direct threat to their identity. First, this was an attack on one of the most sacred sites of Buddhism in the world, if not on Buddhism itself, and to the extent that a Sinhalese person considered him- or herself a Buddhist, this would be an attack on that person's identity. Second, Kandy was the capital of the Sinhalese kings for the period between 1592 and 1815, except for brief periods, and therefore it is at the heart of Sinhalese history. To the extent that being Sinhalese (which nearly all Buddhists in Sri Lanka are) is an important element of a person's identity, an attack on a place that is historically a center of Sinhalese power would be a threat to that identity. The bombing also came during the preparations for celebrating the fiftieth anniversary of Sri Lanka's independence from Britain. And so, to the extent that the person identifies with the nation of Sri Lanka and its self-government, the timing of the attack was also a threat to the integrity of that identity.

Thus, running through these conflicts are issues of identity—defining, protecting, and strengthening the boundaries of identity. Identity is a common theme in the psychological explanations of conflict, and it is also a consistent theme in the case studies. And fortunately, recent work in psychology has laid the groundwork for an understanding of identity that links its individual characteristics with its social (and, in this case, national) nature.

I should note at this point that there are some who might say that identity is not a part of these conflicts at all. Over and over again in Sri Lanka, for example, Sinhalese nationalists told me that the conflict there is not about identity, it is about terrorism. In their view, the problem is not about tensions between Tamils and Sinhalese; it is about a small group of terrorists, funded from abroad, with the tacit consent of the West. It would be foolish to claim that geopolitical and economic factors are absent in this conflict, because they are clearly present. At the same time, though, identity still is central. When a Tamil person is stopped by an army checkpoint in Colombo simply because she is Tamil, that is an identity issue. When the Sri Lankan government set differing standards for university admission for Sinhalese and Tamil students in the early 1970s, that was an identity issue. When Sinhalese Sri Lankan émigrés in the United States express their embarrassment about suspecting that their Tamil neighbors might be LTTE supporters, simply because they are Tamils, that is an identity issue. Similarly, even if economic frustrations were driving the rioters in Sumgait, when Armenians were dragged from their apartments, they were targeted because they were Armenian. Identity issues are certainly not the only factor involved in these conflicts, but they play a prominent role. And as I will argue, a lack of attention to identity issues can significantly impede attempts at understanding and resolving such conflicts.

Personal and Social Identity

As noted at the end of the last chapter, the first task of a cohesive understanding of nationalism is to come up with a way of simultaneously understanding the two central dimensions of nationalism—the individual and the social. This is a problem in all of psychology, not just in understanding nationalism. But because nationalism happens in the context of specific historical, cultural, economic, and political circumstances, it becomes even more important to come up with a framework that neither limits our understanding to individuals, nor excludes individuals from the equation.

Part of this problem comes from the traditional Western approach to understanding identity. In this approach, identity tends to be seen as very much a static property of the individual; our identity (or personality) is considered a bounded kind of entity, an unchanging "I" who travels through situations and relationships. As it turns out, that is not the case. In recent years, an approach to understanding identity known as Social Identity Theory,[2] and a later elaboration called Self-Categorization Theory,[3] have begun to provide a way of dealing with this problem. The first basic suggestion of this approach is that our sense of who we are comes from two different but equally important aspects.

The first is our personal identity, which derives from our individual history and experiences. The second is our social identity, which derives from our membership in various kinds of social groups. The social aspect of our identity is as much a part of any of us as the individual aspect; they are both a part of our very "self." That we identify strongly with groups is self-evident; indeed, that is the point of studying nationalism at all! But the idea here is that group identities are not something separate from us, such as a hat or sweater that we might put on and take off. When we categorize ourselves into a group, in a sense that group becomes a *part* of us. In a competitive situation, if our group loses, *we* lose. If our group wins, *we* win. So in that sense, a competition over resources, for example, might *not* be just about the actual resources that we get or lose. It might be about our own conception of ourselves, as winners or losers. We feel those identities as part of us.

This conception of social identity has an interesting and important implication. Remember that any individual can be part of a variety of "ingroups" at any given time, depending on whom they are comparing themselves to. In my Psychology of Nationalism course, for example, one of the students was a woman, a college student, a member of a group called the "Styxx," a psychology major, and a tennis player, all at the same time. Another one was a man, a college student, the guy in "Three Girls and a Guy," a religious studies major, and an ex-soccer player. All of these potential identities were important to these two individuals, but they were not equally important at all times. During the group work sessions, their memberships in the class groups were most salient, and understandably so. During one session, in fact, this particular member of Three Girls and a Guy was assigned the task of trying to get the Styxx to yell at his group, so he dumped a trash can in Styxx's territory, threw paper airplanes at them, and in general made himself a pest. During that session, the interactions between the two individuals described above were based almost solely on those group identities. However, if these two had met at a fraternity dance party, their interaction would likely have been very different. Their Styxx or Three Girls and a Guy group identities would no longer be salient; instead, their gender identities would be much more important and have far more consequences for them. And if they met on a recruiting trip where they were talking to prospective students about this college, their interactions would again be based on different group identities—this time, their shared group identity as college students.

The point here is that this conception of identity points out a radical truth about who we are. According to this view, identity is not fixed or bounded; there is not a single "me" who is the same from situation to situation. Instead, identity is fluid, responding to a combination of our own needs and of the situation around us. Our actual identity—who we think we are, the way we think of ourselves—is constantly shifting and changing. This conception means we can not talk about identity as independent of the situation we are in, because identity is *simultaneously individual and social*. Different aspects of our identity become more salient depending on the situation. The situation, in a sense, *evokes* different parts of us, makes them more central to us. Thus identity combines both our individual and our social aspects. That is why identity is the best starting point from which to try to understand nationalism.

Naturally, there are some questions that arise. The first would be this: If identity is constantly shifting and changing, why do some identities (such as national identity) seem to be so important for so many people? Are some social identities by nature more "primary" or more important to our sense of self than others? The answer is that no social identity is inherently any more important than any other, but the social circumstances in which we live serve to *reinforce* certain identities—and especially national identity—as being most salient. To make that point, however, we first need to understand the nature and qualities of national identity in some depth.

What Is National Identity?

To begin, what is "national identity" anyway? There are many answers to that question; in fact, defining "the nation" is a central topic in a wide variety of writings in political science and international relations. Anthony Smith, a modern observer of nationalism, gives the fundamental features of a nation as "a named human population sharing an historical territory, common myths and historical memories, a mass public culture, a common economy and common legal rights and duties for all members."[4] This definition focuses on commonality, both in history and current life. The Kurds, a people who are spread through territories belonging to Turkey, Iraq, Iran, and Syria, would not qualify according to this definition; they do not presently have a common economy or set of legal rights. And presumably, according to this definition, the Armenians living in the diaspora, in Syria or Lebanon, would not be considered part of the Armenian nation. The diaspora Armenians and Kurds might object to these characterizations, though, because many of them certainly consider themselves to be members of "nations." This fact suggests that there is more to national identity than physical or economic connections between people. Benedict Anderson, another well-known theorist of nationalism, provides a very different definition, suggesting that the nation is "an imagined political community—and imagined as both inherently limited and sovereign."[5] By "imagined," Anderson does not mean "unreal"; he simply means that nations are communities in which people *believe* there is a connection between them and the other members of that nation, even if they have never actually come into contact with those others (as, indeed, most people in a nation never will). This definition allows for linguistic or ethnic groups that do not actually control their own territory and economic life, but that perhaps have aspirations to do so, to consider themselves "nations," as indeed do many of the Sri Lankan Tamils.

More importantly, Anderson's definition highlights that national identity is not simply racial or territorial or economic or political; it is also psychological. People *identify* themselves with national groups, and that is part of what makes those national groups real. We envision connections between ourselves and the rest of that national group. These connections do not have to be historically "true"; they simply need to be psychologically real.

National Narratives

One primary way in which we envision this connection between us and the other members of our nation is through shared stories of the origin and experiences of our people, or what might be termed "national narratives."[6] For example, the history of Buddhism in Sri Lanka is told in a set of monastic chronicles, the most important of which is the Mahavamsa, or "The Great Chronicle." These narratives, written in an ancient language called Pali, identify the history of Buddhism with the history of the Sinhalese people.[7] For example, in one passage, the Buddha is lying on his deathbed and speaking to an assembly of gods with his final requests. The Buddha says:

> Vijaya, son of king Sihabahu, is come to Lanka from the country of Lala, together with seven hundred followers. In Lanka, O lord of gods, will my religion be established, therefore carefully protect him with his followers and Lanka.[8]

Thus in this story, the Buddha designates the island of Sri Lanka as the home for Buddhism. As a result, Sinhalese nationalists now assert that they must protect Buddhism by giving it the primary religious role in Sri Lanka.[9] However, the chronicles go on to tell of the difficulty of protecting Buddhism over the centuries because of invasion after invasion by Tamils.[10] One of the most often cited passages by both Sinhalese nationalists and their opponents is a passage about an interchange between Dutthagamani, a Sinhalese king who lived in the second century B.C.E., and some of the monks with whom he kept counsel. After a particularly fierce battle, in which Dutthagamani's armies killed "millions" of his Tamil opponents, Dutthagamani feels remorse over the carnage. He confesses this to the monks, who are said to have replied:

> From this deed arises no hindrance in thy way to heaven. Only one and a half human beings have been slain here by thee, O lord of men. The one had come unto the (three) refuges, the other had taken on himself the five precepts. [Note: these are stages in accepting the Buddhist way of life.] Unbelievers and men of evil life were the rest, not more to be esteemed than beasts. But as for thee, thou wilt bring glory to the doctrine of the Buddha in manifold ways; therefore cast away care from thy heart, O ruler of men![11]

The portrait that this text provides, of Tamils as unworthy of any more care than beasts, would certainly be disputed by many Buddhists in Sri Lanka and elsewhere. But the general point is that such stories play two functions for Sinhalese Buddhist identity. First, they give a sense of common history and common purpose to the Sinhalese people. And second, they provide an "other" against which the Sinhalese can define themselves, a group to contrast themselves against when they are shaping their own sense of identity.[12]

Most nations have narratives like this that they tell about themselves. Often they describe significant social or political events in the group's history, such as the Boston Tea Party in the United States, in which colonists are said to have dumped tea into Boston Harbor in 1773 in protest of taxation by the British without representation; or the story of the "Great Trek" in South Africa in the mid-nineteenth century, in which thousands of Afrikaners left the Cape Town colony to find better pastures further north. The events most remembered may be great triumphs or, as we will see in chapter 5, great traumas or disasters. Both help to define a people's sense of who they are.

The narratives themselves can be transmitted in various ways. Sometimes they are enshrined in religious documents or scriptures such as the *Mahavamsa* or the Hebrew Bible. Often they are told as stories through films, novels, and other cultural materials. And, of course, they are transmitted through textbooks that are used in history curricula in schools. Interestingly, in some cases the "official" and "unofficial" versions of a nation's history may clash. In Estonia before the breakup of the Soviet Union, schools taught a version of Estonian history that emphasized the 1940 "socialist revolution" in Estonia but systematically excluded information about Estonian political leaders and positive social events during Estonia's years of independence (1917-1940). Families, however, continued to tell the banned stories of Estonian nationhood, and those stories were the ones that remained in the consciousness of Estonians.[13]

In fact, the competing versions of historical narratives can often play a central role in nationalist conflict, particularly when they deal with the justification of a group's grievances or its holding of territory. "Who was here first?" is a common question that national historical narratives answer. For example, consider these competing stories of the origin of Sri Lanka:

During this period of 1,500 years [500 B.C.E.-993 A.D.] a single tribe known as the Sinhalas, who were of North Indian origin, succeeded in establishing a centralized administrative system, with the capital at Anuradhapura, in North Central Sri Lanka. . . . There is no historical evidence to prove that any Dravidian (Tamil) settlements existed in Sri Lanka during this period. If there were Dravidians (Tamils) in the country during this period, it is quite likely that they were Buddhists, like the main bulk of the Tamils who were in South India at the time, and would have been absorbed into the Sinhala identity during this 1500 year period.[14]

The Tamils are the indigenous people of Ceylon. Their history had its beginnings in the early settlements on the rich alluvial plains near the southern extremity of the peninsular India. The Tamils were sea faring people. They traded with Rome in the days of Emperor Augustus. They sent ships to many lands bordering the Indian Ocean and with the ships went traders, scholars and a way of life. The island of Ceylon which was separated from the Indian subcontinent by less than 30 miles of water was not unknown to the Tamils who called it Eelam and who established their early kingdoms there more than 3,000 years ago.[15]

The excerpt on the left comes from a Sinhalese nationalist source, whereas the one on the right comes from a Tamil nationalist source. The contrasting views of history are quite clear. Each one lays claim to being there first. The Sinhalese source even goes a bit further, suggesting that if there were Tamils in Sri Lanka early on, they probably became Sinhalese anyway. These competing versions of history play a role in the arguments about who is rightly the heir of the island today, and these arguments can be very contentious. Both sides present historical and archeological evidence to demonstrate their claims, and both sides believe that their version is correct.

That there are sometimes competing versions of these narratives is not strange. In fact, scholars have paid a significant amount of attention in recent years to the way in which national groups often "invent" histories or traditions that serve to link their members together. One notable example is that of the "highland tradition of Scotland." Hugh Trevor-Roper has argued persuasively that many of the features of "traditional" Scottish identity, including the bagpipe, the kilt, and the tartan, are in fact comparatively modern. The kilt, in fact, was invented by an English Quaker named Thomas Rawlinson in the 1720s![16] But whether or not historical narratives are literally true is not the central point; moreover, in many (or even most) cases, that is impossible to determine. The importance is that such stories are one of the central defining features of national identity, and they can play heavily into nationalist conflict.[17] Indeed, history was very often the first topic of conversation that my interviewees initiated in Armenia and Azerbaijan, where there is a divergence of stories similar to that in Sri Lanka about who "originally" lived in Nagorno-Karabakh. Those I met were eager to tell me about the monuments, poets, and national treasures found in Nagorno-Karabakh, which demonstrated to them the essential Armenian-ness or Azerbaijani-ness of Nagorno-Karabakh's territory.[18]

Those engaged in nationalist movements, of course, understand the importance of history. That is why the Soviet Union banned the teaching of Armenian history in Nagorno-Karabakh schools in 1987 (an act that later had consequences for Armenians' justification of the Nagorno-Karabakh movement). Teaching history is sometimes tantamount to asserting a national identity, and states often attempt to create a unified and "official" history that is then propagated through school curricula.[19] But there is more. Controversies arise about the teaching of history not only because history is tied up with politics and nationalism in conflicts between national groups, but also because national identity is not static; it constantly shifts and changes.

The Changing Nature of National Identity

One explanation for why ethnic conflict has broken out in places such as Bosnia, Chechnya, Nagorno-Karabakh, and other areas of the former Soviet Union and Eastern Europe is that many of these peoples had long-standing ethnic rivalries and hatreds, and the authoritarian Soviet system simply swept those antagonisms under the carpet half a century ago and kept them under control. Now that the Soviet system has fallen apart, those national sentiments, and the national animosities that accompany them, are simply rearing their heads again. (Some have termed this the "carpet theory."[20]) Such an idea ignores a whole range of historical and other factors, such as how the Soviet Union influenced national identity and ethnicity by moving large ethnic populations away from their homelands, and manipulating language policies in the schools of the various republics. But more importantly, this idea suggests that national identity is fixed and unchanging; that it is always clear who is, or is not, a member of a national group; and that those criteria and the self-understanding of such groups do not change through historical circumstances.

However, the opposite may well be true. National identities may undergo a constant process of change. For example, when scholars attempt to explain how the Sri Lankan conflict came about and why it persists, they seem to tell two basic stories.[21] The first, similar to the carpet theory, suggests that the Sinhalese and the Tamils are historical enemies who have been fighting each other for many centuries, and thus today's conflict is simply the modern expression of that historical enmity. Some use the stories in the *Mahavamsa* to bolster that claim—either viewing Sinhalese national identity as resulting from centuries of attacks by Tamils, or viewing Tamil national identity as resulting from centuries of Sinhalese attempts to deny the Tamils their rightful heritage on the island.

However, a very different explanation for the conflict says it is rooted not in ancient history but in more recent history—specifically, the experience of Sri Lanka under British colonialism, from 1796 to 1948. This argument suggests that while there were separate Tamil and Sinhalese communities on the island for centuries, they actually got along reasonably well most of the time and did not see themselves as particularly different. In fact, there was (and is) no inherent reason why Buddhists and Hindus might not be able to live next to each other and even participate in each other's religious ceremonies.[22] When Protestant missionaries from England arrived in the 1800s, they found little religious antagonism on the island. However, those missionaries expected that religions *should* be in conflict with each other, and should compete for souls; this was the missionaries' understanding of Christianity. By pitting Christianity against Buddhism (using debates and drives for converts), this argument goes, they essentially *taught* the Sinhalese to be intolerant.[23] The British also created social and economic discrepancies between the two groups by giving Tamils a more prominent place in government employment and the professions.[24] The Sinhalese, in particular, reacted to these threats by attempting to bolster their own national identity, and the Tamils in turn did the same in response to the growing Sinhalese nationalism. In the process, both groups developed antagonistic national identities that did not exist before.[25] The conclusion of this argument is that, to the extent that Sinhalese-Tamil enmity exists on any kind of broad scale, it is essentially a modern creation; and that those artificially constructed identities, which were first fueled by historical inequities and now by the ideology of the pure nation-state, have produced the current intractable conflict.

There have been similar continuing explorations of Armenian identity occurring over the last couple of centuries. Since Armenia is a nation whose members have long been spread out over several continents, the question of who is and who is not Armenian, and perhaps who is and who is not an Armenian nationalist or patriot, takes on special intensity. There is an Armenian language and an Armenian Orthodox Church, and there are lands that the Armenians traditionally consider theirs. However, many members of the Armenian diaspora no longer speak Armenian, and many others do not practice the Armenian Orthodox faith; and, by definition, they all live outside the borders of the current Republic of Armenia. How should "Armenian-ness" be defined? One long-standing student of Armenia suggests that, for many, being an Armenian nationalist is sometimes seen to be what makes one a "true" Armenian.[26]

So national identities may well evolve and change in response to social conditions surrounding the peoples involved. National identities may also evolve and change through explicit efforts. In Azerbaijan, a number of scholars have made efforts in recent years to develop a history of the Azerbaijani people that connects them definitively to Nagorno-Karabakh and the surrounding areas. That effort focuses on the history of a people known as the "Albanians" (not related to the Albanians in the Balkans) who are said to have inhabited the area that is now Armenia and Azerbaijan for many centuries. Azerbaijani scholars have claimed that the modern-day Azerbaijanis, as well as many other of the national groups who live in Azerbaijan (and perhaps even the Armenians, too) are descendants of the Albanians, and that is one reason why Azerbaijani claims to Nagorno-Karabakh are justified. Something that would, in most cases, be an academic exercise in ancient history has become, for the Azerbaijanis and the Armenians, a thorny issue with real and immediate application. The scholar who began the movement to study Albania, Ziya Buniayatov, was shot and stabbed in 1997 by unknown assassins.[27] National identity, and the stories that make it up, are sometimes a battleground.

So national identity shifts and changes over time. However, other kinds of social identity might, too. Why does nationalism in particular evoke such passion and dedication among so many people? Is there something "primary" about it?

Why National Identity?

As I noted at the beginning of this chapter, there are many potential social groups that any of us might identify with at any given time. From a psychological point of view, there is nothing "primal" about national identity—no obvious reason why national identity should evoke any stronger passion or closer identification than other forms of social identity. [28] In fact, as I noted in chapter 1, ingroup-outgroup phenomena can develop across any kind of difference, so that the same kinds of ingroup favoritism and outgroup devaluation can in principle (and do, indeed, in practice) develop between Israelis and Palestinians, Hatfields and McCoys, the Gatekeepers and the Smooth Operators, the Jets and the Sharks. There are even times when people actually do risk their lives for other kinds of group affiliations, such as in gang conflicts or conflicts between labor and management, or in class-based revolutions. So on the face of it, national identity, as a variety of social identity, is not different from any other variety.

And yet national identity does play a special role, at least in the world as it now is. Political leaders who speak of nations as if they are the most important form of social organization, to be protected and fought for, do not even feel the need to justify this assertion.[29] Looking around the globe, we can easily find many nationalist movements, from East Timor to Tibet. Indeed, the ubiquity of nationalism is the reason for writing this book. So why might national identity, among all the various kinds of social groups with which people might identify, play such a prominent role in our current time?

In political science a great deal of work has been done to address this question. The answers often take the form of a debate between those scholars known as "primordialists" and those known as "modernists."[30] The primordialists argue that national identity is connected to ethnic identity and is essential to our nature. In contrast, the modernists suggest that, because of a range of historical factors such as the need for a centralized workforce and the expansion of literacy, nationalism—in the sense of a group identification that is directed toward the establishment or predominance of a nation-state—is essentially a modern phenomenon.

In psychology there are also theoretical approaches that highlight the role of current social and political history in attempting to understand the primacy of nationalism. One argument is that in Eastern Europe and the former Soviet Union, for example, when the stable structure of the Cold War broke down, people might have begun searching for a new way of understanding themselves, with nationalism providing a sense of meaning to fill that void.[31] The major problem with this point of view is that, although it seems to fit the situation of the former Soviet Union pretty well, it does not appear to explain the nationalism in Sri Lanka, much less that of the United States—which while not so obvious as in other areas of the world, is nonetheless evident in many ways.[32] And why would national identity provide such meaning more than any other social identity? Can it provide something that other forms of group identity cannot? National groups are almost always associated with a territory, and having a sense of place could provide a kind of security that other forms of group identity do not. However, other forms of group identity *do* fill this need. A gang, for example, often controls a territory. College fraternities typically own houses in which the members live, which form a central part of their identity. In addition, national groups can provide a sense of destiny. But one's destiny may well be more immediately linked to the fortunes of the company one works for than to the national group. So what is so special about nationalism?

To answer this question, we first have to remember that our identities are constantly shifting. The question we are asking is not why national identity is so important in isolation, as if it needs to be evaluated against all other possible kinds of social identity. Instead, we are asking why national identity is so important to particular groups of people, at particular times, in today's world. For example, I have already noted that the salience of various social identities changes. The Styxx and Three Girls and a Guy identities of the two students in my Psychology of Nationalism class were most in their consciousness when the two groups were feuding, whereas the two students' gender identities would be primary when they saw each other at a party. Similarly, the social identities of people in real-world conflicts shift, too. One of the most puzzling phenomena in the modern world has been that people who previously lived peacefully with one another can suddenly turn on each other with brutality and ferocity. In Bosnia, for example, Bosnian Croats, Bosnian Muslims, and Bosnian Serbs lived in many of the same villages and even intermarried for many years. Yet when Yugoslavia began to fall apart, in many cases they turned on each other with brutality.[33] Similar phenomena happened during the 1983 riots Sri Lanka, in which Sinhalese mobs attacked Tamils. Those two groups had lived largely peacefully side by side in Colombo and the surrounding areas before the riots, and indeed, have done so since the riots to the present day, even as the conflict has raged in the north and east of the island. As I mentioned before, social identities shift in their salience depending on both our own history (our identification with those groups) and the social context.[34] At one time a citizenship-based national identity might be primary, at another time a more ethnically-based national identity might be primary, and at yet another time religious identity might be primary. But what specific features of the social context produce such changes?

The answer comes from two sources. First, we need to turn back to Social Identity Theory again. Social Identity Theory assumes that we are all constantly striving to improve our self-concept—our sense of how valuable we are. (I will examine that assumption in the next chapter.) Our evaluation of ourselves is inherently comparative, in that when we want to assess how good we are, the primary way to do so is to look at other individuals and social groups and see how we line up. So when faced with an array of social groups with which to identify (a process that does not need to take place consciously), we will tend to identify most with the group that provides the best opportunity to promote a positive sense of social identity.[35]

Let me explain this in terms of the studies that inspired these ideas, many of which were conducted by Henri Tajfel and his colleagues.[36] For example, in one series of studies, high school students were put in a room and shown a series of pairs of abstract paintings by Paul Klee and Vasily Kandinsky. After each pair of paintings, the researchers asked the students (who did not know which painting was from which painter) to choose the one from each pair that they liked best. At the end the researchers collected the answer sheets, tabulated them, and then went around and indicated privately to each student that he or she was in the group that preferred Klee or the group that preferred Kandinsky. (The assigning of the students to the two groups was totally arbitrary and not based on the students' preferences, though the students did not know that.) Then the researchers gave the participants, individually, an opportunity to allocate money to the others who had taken part in the research, knowing only whether those individuals were in the Klee group or the Kandinsky group. Very predictably over many studies, and over many different ways of assigning the groups, the participants gave more money to the people who were like them (in the same group) than those who were different. In fact, when the system of allocating rewards was made more complex, and participants had the opportunity to assign money so as either to maximize their own group's profit or to maximize the *difference* between their group's success and that of the comparison group (even if their own group got a smaller total of money), the students often chose to maximize the differences between the groups.[37] In none of these situations did the participants benefit individually from the money; all of this had to do with their allocation of money to others.

These results have been replicated with the choice of paintings, the estimate of a number of quickly flashed dots, and even a flip of the coin as the determiner of who was in which group. The actual differences between the groups were nonexistent. So it turns out that we do not need real differences between people to create ingroup-outgroup phenomena. All we need is the *perception* that there are group differences, and people begin to *identify* with "their" group enough to favor it and to penalize the "outgroup."

This is a strange and counterintuitive result. Why would people identify with an essentially arbitrary group distinction and favor that new "ingroup," when they had so many other group identities that they might identify with instead? John C. Turner, one of the primary proponents of this approach, explains it by saying:

> Where an intergroup situation allows a positive self-evaluation on *some* dimension, then the individual confronting this situation will define himself in social terms relevant to that dimension.[38]

What this means is that if we are always searching for *any* way to value ourselves more positively, then we will reach, even unconsciously, for the social identity that will give us the best chance to do so. In the experimental situation, the participants had many other potential social identities to identify with. But in providing them with two distinctively different groups, and then providing them with a way of valuing the groups (the money that was given out), the researchers created a situation in which the minimal groups that had been created were the most salient. This gave participants a way of increasing their positive social identity, and so each one identified with a group, and favored it.

The relevance of this research to nationalism is this: If identifying with a national group provides an opportunity for positively valuing ourselves, then we will identify with that national group—in other words, we will experience nationalism. And does national identity provide us with more opportunities for positive social evaluation? The answer is that in our current world context, it does. And it does so for several reasons. First, internationally recognized countries hold a high value because they are able to give citizenship, receive international aid, and sit in the United Nations;

these are powerful marks of status in our world.[39] Therefore a national group that is striving to establish an independent state would be potentially valuable to identify with, because it may achieve these markers of status vis-à-vis other national groups.

Perhaps equally as important, in our international system we use a rhetoric that privileges self-determination of national groups. National struggles are given higher status than political or class struggles, for example; the right of self-determination is included in the U.N. Charter and the Helsinki Final Act. This means that in terms of international respect, and perhaps also in terms of being able to receive military or other aid, it is valuable to identify with a national group and its concomitant historical, territorial, and emotional associations. The United States and other Western countries have used this rhetoric of self-determination to suggest that other peoples ought to become independent (that is, to identify themselves with nationalist movements), particularly during the period of the breakup of the Soviet Union. (Of course, in other contexts, the United States has insisted on the importance of maintaining established borders.) And rebel groups use this rhetoric now as a principle on which to ground their struggles. The LTTE's headquarters in London, for example, explains their case by saying:

> The Tamil people of the island of Ceylon (now called Sri Lanka) constitute a distinct nation. They form a social entity, with their own history, traditions, culture, language and traditional homeland. The Tamil people call their nation "Tamil Eelam."
>
> As a nation, Tamils have the inalienable right to self-determination, a universal principle enshrined in the U.N. Charter that guarantees the right of a people to political independence.[40]

Obviously, the LTTE, as well as existing states such as the United States and others, may use this rhetoric to further their own interests. Nationalist leaders in separatist struggles may do so too, to garner support for their cause, to rally their own people, or simply to keep a conflict going so as to enrich themselves. That is the point of nationalist propaganda, after all. So the promulgation of the value of nationalism does not necessarily imply that people believe it is the best way to proceed. What it suggests is why we *respond* to such appeals. This valuing of nationalism in international and domestic public discourses makes national identity a way to provide a positive social identity. If people perceive that a particular kind of group identity will enhance their self-esteem, they will identify with it, particularly when they are suffering economic or social deprivation that diminishes their sense of self-esteem.[41] And so we do.

Threat

There is one other way in which a particular social identity might become salient, and that is threat: If a particular social identity is threatened, it becomes salient. When the group Arcadia was criticized in class for having one of their members fake nausea to get out of the room, their identity as Arcadia became more meaningful to them. Similarly, if a Tamil is stopped at a checkpoint in Colombo simply because she is Tamil, then her "Tamilness" is likely to feel most meaningful to her. Threat to national identities is common in our world, partially because of the very reasons described above—national identities are in some ways the battleground of social comparison. When we evaluate the worth of our national identity, we do so by comparing it to the status of other national identities. If we can denigrate those others, or threaten them in some way, our social identity is comparatively better.

Threats to national identity can be direct or symbolic. The threat to Tamils during the 1983 riots in Colombo was very real and very direct; Tamils were targeted simply because of their national identity. The bombing of the Temple of the Tooth, described earlier, threatened all Sinhalese indirectly because of the centrality of that temple to Sinhalese culture and history. Even the situation of the Azerbaijani scholars' searching for their roots in Caucasian Albania could be interpreted as a threat to Armenians, because it challenged the legitimacy of Armenian claims to what they see as their traditional homelands. There is also experimental research that suggests that when individuals experience threat based on some aspect of their identity, they increase the degree to which they feel that aspect is important.[42]

Overall, we affiliate with national identities because they provide us with a way of improving our self-concept, and others target our national identities for threat because they, in turn, are trying to improve their own self-concept. Changes in the social–political context, such as a potential bid for independence or a threat to some aspect of our integrity as a people, intensify that identification. With this idea we can begin to see why the nation inspires such devotion in the current world context. Nationhood is in many ways the currency of self-worth, and the more it is trumpeted as the natural, most important, and most respected form of social identity, the more we will cling to that identity in our daily sense of ourselves.

This way of thinking about national identity fits the facts of nationalism better than does positing the awakening of some long-dormant but static national antagonisms. It also suggests that in another context, other kinds of identity (religious or ethnic identity, for example) could serve the same function. For example, in a time when it was believed that salvation was the most important goal of life, rather than self-determination, we would expect religious identity to have been more important than national identity—as indeed it was in Europe during much of the Middle Ages. At other times, class identity has been seen as the most important way of gaining a sense of self-respect and self-worth, and then we would expect class identity to be people's most salient social identity, as indeed it has been during class revolutions around the world. Similarly, people sometimes shift from valuing a citizenship-based sense of nationhood to an ethnic one, as has happened in Bosnia and Rwanda. This approach takes into account the shifting nature of identity that is so evident in our daily lives. And given the international system as it now stands, this approach helps us understand why national identity, at this time, would seem to be so popular a way to identify ourselves, even in those areas of the world that do not have the Western European history of building nation-states.

The Missing Link

I have argued in this chapter that identity is made up of social and personal components, and that identifying with a nation is, in our day and age, one of the most important ways that we can increase our self-regard. There is a good deal of experimental evidence that supports the view that social identities can change and that national identity, in particular, is tied clearly to the social context in which it is being experienced. Far from being static historical entities, national identities are always evolving and changing in response to the historical and social circumstances in which they are found.

A major assumption of this approach, as I have mentioned above, is that we all constantly strive for a positive sense of ourselves.[43] If we accept the assumption that we are always striving for positive social identity—which we gain, at least in part, by comparing the fortunes and status of our group with those of other groups—then the reasons for ingroup favoritism, outgroup devaluation, and intergroup conflict all become more clear. Valuing our own group more highly than others (ingroup favoritism), and denigrating other groups (outgroup devaluation) make a lot of sense; both these approaches serve to increase our sense of self-worth. In addition, as argued above, if national identity provides a good way to compare ourselves with others and hence to increase our evaluation of ourselves, then, given the current political discourse in the world, national identity would be a very salient form of social identity to promote in ourselves. Thus nationalism might serve an important function for us—to help us increase our self-esteem.

But several questions remain unanswered: Why should we always need to strive for a positive sense of identity? What is wrong with us the way we are? What is it about the nature of identity that leads us to be striving constantly to improve it? And even if devaluing others plays a role for us, why do people so often do it with such brutality and vehemence? After all, to devalue another group, all we have to do is to say that they are bad or worthless; we do not need to rape or kill them, or to mutilate their bodies after they are dead. By focusing on identity we have found a unit of analysis that will help us understand the intertwining personal, cultural, and historical aspects of nationalism. But for that unit of analysis to be adequate, we have to understand the more emotional issues, too. And in order to do so, we will have to take a deeper look at the nature of identity.

Chapter 4

THE FRAGILITY
OF IDENTITY

Assuming that people are constantly trying to improve their self-esteem helps us understand a number of the common aspects of nationalism. We identify strongly with a nation because, in today's world, national identity offers us the greatest possibilities for increasing our sense of self-worth. We devalue other national groups because, when we compare ourselves to them, we feel more important, more moral, and more just. But why should we constantly be striving to increase our self-esteem? Is there something wrong with us?

To answer these questions we will have to examine the most basic facts of human existence. We need to explore how we as humans deal with both the glorious and the painful realities of life. And when we look at those realities and our response to them, we will find two phenomena that, I would suggest, underlie much of nationalism. The first is that we fear we are fragile. The second is that we are unwilling to accept aspects of ourselves because we are ashamed of them. Nationalism is one way we can attempt to deal with these fundamental challenges to our identity.

In this chapter I will argue that these are two of the basic underlying concerns of our lives, and that they are relevant for both personal and national identity. In chapter 5, we will see how they play out in the broader realm of nationalist movements. The truth of these assertions does not rest simply in argumentation, however. Because we will be dealing with fundamental experiences that we as humans have, each of us will have to consider whether or not these assertions make sense in the context of our own lives. Once we do so, we may well find that the processes that underlie nationalism are operating in our own experience too.

Personal Identity Is Fragile

At first glance, it may seem strange to assert that we fear we are fragile. After all, human beings are vital and resilient in many ways. We have produced great accomplishments, from dams and bridges to literature and art; and medical care (at least, for those in the world with access to it) is increasing our life spans every year.

And yet at the individual level, we are fragile. Each of us carries with us the knowledge that at any time, we could cease to exist. We could get sick; we could get hit by a bus. Simply by the nature of being human, we are at risk of dying. That is a reality, and although there are things we can do to hasten death (reckless behavior, for example) or to try to put it off (exercise and good self-care), there is nothing we can do to take away the risk of dying. It could happen at any moment, and we would cease to be.

Equally as importantly, we also face the possibility that *psychologically* we could cease to exist at any time, because the integrity of our identity is also always at risk. Here in the West we tend to take "identity" as a given, believing that we have a coherent and bounded identity that is consistent from moment to moment and situation to situation.[1] And yet it seems clear, as I argued in the previous chapter, that the reality of identity is more complex than that. The "self" is partially defined by our relationships with others, and our conception of ourselves shifts and changes depending on the social context—what is happening around us, both in our immediate situation and even, potentially, far away. The self is neither coherent nor consistent.

But if the self is not bounded and unique, why do we think it is? After all, U.S. society, in particular, has a very strong thread of individualism running through it; we tend to see ourselves "rugged individuals" working our way through the world. But it may be that we believe in the primacy of the individual self not because it corresponds to reality, but simply because we are taught to do so. Roy Baumeister, a psychologist, has written a series of articles and books on the "self" as seen in Western society[2] in which he makes exactly this point. For example, in a situation familiar to most parents, a parent might offer a child a tuna fish sandwich. The child says she does not like tuna fish. The parent might then reply, "What do you mean you don't like tuna fish? You liked it last time!" The implication, of course, is that if you liked it last time, you should also like it this time—because people are consistent. In actual fact, consistency is not necessarily the natural order of children's behavior, as any parent knows. But the parent's continued insistence that there ought to be consistency in an individual over time gives the child the message that there should be an inner "self" that is the same, that has preferences and continuity across time and situations. The same principle applies if a child does something against the rules. If a parent tells a child not to draw on the walls, and the child goes ahead and does it anyway, the parent might ask "Why did you draw on the wall when I told you not to do it? Why?" A young child may well be unable to answer that question; it takes time before we are able to understand our own motivations. But if the parent continues to ask those kinds of questions about why the child does what she does, eventually the child will figure out that when you do things, it is because there is some inner state, inner self, that makes you do it. In essence, Baumeister argues, we *teach* the child that there is a "self" that is in control of her actions. Do that enough times, and we will finally begin to get the child to talk in a language we grown-ups understand, a language of rational behavior, of inner states that lead to action, of reasons for what they do (even though they may not be the ones the parents want!).

So the concept that we each have a strong and bounded identity may simply be the way we are taught to think about ourselves and not the way things "really" are. And indeed there is growing evidence that our identities are not as strong as we thought, and that we are frantically trying to shore them up. Psychological research is filled with attempts to study the "self," to find out when it appears, how it changes during the "identity crisis" of adolescence, and whether or not it holds together in old age. Bookstores have shelves filled with self-help books designed to help us increase our self-esteem,[3] and schools have at times turned to curricula that are supposed to focus on the development of children's sense of self.[4] My favorite example of our increasing focus on the self came during a reunion concert of the folk group "Peter, Paul, and Mary" several years ago. In reminiscing over the many years since they first started singing together, one of the group commented that times have changed: One of the most popular magazines used to be *Life*. Then there was one called *People*. Then there was one called *Us*. Now we see one called *Self*. And it is true. Self-knowledge, self-esteem, and self-fulfillment seem to be major preoccupations of current American society.

My point here is not to condemn such a focus on the self, as some have done.[5] I am simply pointing out that all of this focus on the self suggests that at some level, we think something is wrong. We seem to believe that without special attention, our sense of self will falter or fail. We seem to believe that our identities are fragile. I would argue that we spend so much time studying, analyzing, and trying to shape "the self" because at some level we recognize that it is not nearly as stable a phenomenon as we believe.

And this is to be expected. Because the entire concept that we each have a separate and unique identity is only one way, and a fairly recent one, of looking at the self. First of all, the Western idea that each person is an integrated and separate whole is a relatively uncommon idea, if one looks around the world.[6] Some peoples tend to describe each other by focusing not on internal states or personality "traits," but instead by describing how they act in certain situations, or how their behavior affects other people.[7] Second, this focus on the self is fairly modern, having developed only over the last several hundred years.[8] Interestingly, however, even though the United States fixates on the "self" in a way that other societies do not, other societies deal with the same issue in other ways. Traditional Theravada Buddhism (practiced in Sri Lanka), for example, explicitly addresses the concept of the self by *denying* that there is an unchanging self that somehow underlies all of our actions and experiences. Instead, it offers the doctrine of "no-self."[9] An illustration might come from Vipassana meditation, which is practiced in the Theravada Buddhist tradition.[10] Meditation in this tradition is simply observing experience as closely as possible to find out what is really happening. The meditator sits and observes every feeling and experience that occurs. If I am meditating and feel pain, they say, I will first conceptualize it as "my leg is hurting." But if I pay close enough attention, I will find that what I conceptualize as "pain" is really just sensations, that are flowing, changing, never the same from moment to moment; I will also eventually find that what I conceptualize as "my leg" is the same, just a set of sensations that never stop changing. Ultimately, they say, there is no "my leg"; it is all simply a set of effervescent and fleeting sensations. In this view, if we spend enough time looking at, listening to, and experiencing reality, we will find that nothing is as solid and permanent as it looks or feels, including the self. Everything is simply a series of sensations.

This idea can be difficult to accept. Conceptualizing ourselves as unbounded and endlessly changing begins to feel like not existing at all! Indeed, one of the most prominent translators of Buddhism in our time, Walpola Rahula, argues that this doctrine is so difficult for some people to accept that they keep trying to *inject* the "self" into Buddhism when it is translated and understood in the modern world.[11] Why is it so difficult? The answer returns to where we began: Coming into contact with the reality that the self is unbounded reminds us of the real, immediate possibility of not existing. And any contact we have with that possibility causes us anxiety. The Christian theologian Paul Tillich describes our reaction to the threat of "nonbeing" this way:

> The anxiety of fate and death is most basic, most universal, and inescapable. All attempts to argue it away are futile. Even if the so-called arguments for the "immortality of the soul" had argumentative power (which they do not have) they would not convince existentially. For existentially everybody is aware of the complete loss of self which biological extinction implies. . . . Nonbeing is omnipresent and produces anxiety even where an immediate threat of death is absent.[12]

Tillich's point here is that nonbeing, the psychological reality of the ending of our existence, is always present and always causes us anxiety. If there is any experiential reality to Social Identity Theory and Buddhism and other systems of understanding that say that the unitary "self" is a fiction, and if in fact we know at some level that we are not solid, independent beings, then that understanding must at some level inform and guide our actions. Just as the reality of non-being is present for all of us at all times, as Tillich argues above, the knowledge that our "self" is fragile must also cause us anxiety. As I will argue in chapter 5, nationalism is one response to this anxiety that is inherent in being human.

National Identities Are Fragile

Before we can consider our reactions to the fragility of our personal identities, we need to recognize that social identities, including national identity, are just as fragile as personal ones, because they are all to some degree consciously constructed. Although this might be easier to see with an identity that seems "chosen," like that of a fan of a particular baseball team, than with one that seems more "primal," like racial identity, it is equally true of both.

Consider ethnic identity for Jews. Religion is not the only criterion for whether or not someone might consider him- or herself Jewish. Certainly religious practice can be important, but there are many who consider themselves Jewish, in Israel and around the world, who are not practicing Jews. How, then, do they know they are Jewish? Traditionally, Jews hold that identity is passed through the mother.[13] Therefore, if my mother is Jewish, I am Jewish too, even if I grew up in a situation in which Jewish practice was absent. In that sense, Jewish identity is ethnically based, via lineage.

In practice, however, this issue has become complex. If a Jewish woman converts to Christianity and then has children, are her children Jewish? Or if a Christian woman converts to Judaism, are her children Jewish? If a Jewish man marries a non-Jewish woman, can his children be Jewish? These are all questions with which the Israeli religious and secular authorities have had to grapple as they decide who can be a fit marriage partner for a Jew and who can be a citizen of Israel. The point is that attempting to make even a relatively straightforward distinction about an ethnic or religious identity (in this case, Jew versus non-Jew) quickly leads to very difficult complexities.

This point is seen even more starkly if we consider whether or not a person is considered African-American. Racial identity would seem to be immutable, but it too is constructed by peoples and societies. In the United States, various rules have been used to determine if someone should be considered "black." In some states, the rule has been that anyone who is one-fourth or one-eighth black is a black person. Louisiana adopted a rule in 1970 that defined someone as black if he or she was more than one-thirty-second black, but a more common principle was (and is) the "one-drop" rule, which means that a person with any traceable African ancestry at all would be considered black.[14] In more recent times, controversy has erupted about how to classify mixed-race people for purposes of the 2000 census.

The point is that ethnic and racial identities, while "real" in the sense that people feel them and classify themselves and others on the basis of them, are socially constructed and are not "naturally" occurring. In that way they are also open for change. The same is true of many other kinds of social identities. Gender, for example, would seem to be a social identity that is immutable. Even if we leave out, for the moment, people who are transgendered or whose anatomy makes their categorization uncertain, the *identity* of a person as male or female is quite subject to social influence. Even in an age in which employment is becoming less gender-specific, men and women who take jobs that are atypical for their sex (such as male midwives or female military officers) have to deal with the confusion that their choice of occupation creates in others; they may also receive disapproval from others. Such social pressure may in turn serve as a threat to their conception of themselves as male or female.[15]

Thus, to suggest that national identities are constructed is not necessarily a radical claim. Given the particular issues involved in national conflict, however, it makes sense to examine the constructed qualities of national identity in more detail. At the most basic level, there are some national identities that have simply been created artificially. East Germany, for example, had no independent existence as a state or a nation before World War II, nor has it since 1990. In an earlier era, much the same happened when the Spanish empire in Latin America fell apart. Between 1826 and 1850, new countries such as Venezuela and Chile had to search for ways to organize their political systems and economies, which had been divided along the lines of colonial administration. Those national identities such as "Peruvian" or "Uruguayan" that may now seem immutable in fact developed only over the past 175 years, sometimes with the explicit goal of using the nation-state model developed in Europe. Much the same is true of states in Africa, which were also created along the lines of colonial administration. And there was no "American" identity prior to the colonization of North America, just as there is no "Soviet" identity now.

The importance of this argument is that just as personal identities are constructed, so are national identities. And if personal identities have the potential to fall apart, because they are in some sense artificial, the same is true of national identities. Thus I would argue that we feel, experientially, the fragility of our national identities, particularly in times of threat.

Threats of Annihilation

One of the reasons that we feel our national identities to be in danger of falling apart is that there are many ways to threaten them. In the last chapter I described the LTTE bombing of the Temple of the Tooth, which seems to have been an explicit attempt to attack Sinhalese identity. Such threats to identity happen in many ways in nationalist conflicts around the world. Sometimes they are threats to the physical survival of a people; at other times, as in the case of the Temple of the Tooth attack, they are more symbolic. But each attack on the physical or cultural identity of a people contributes to the sense that national identity is fragile.

The experience of Armenians in the Ottoman Empire provides one example. In the late 1800s large numbers of Armenians lived in the Ottoman Empire, many of them in Eastern Anatolia, which is a region close to current-day Armenia. Due to a number of political circumstances, these Armenians began to agitate for more territorial autonomy and formed political parties. The government attempted to suppress these movements, and that provoked several armed uprisings by Armenians. In response to those uprisings, Turkish troops and Kurds killed more than 50,000 Armenians in 1894 and 1896.[16] A number of years later, during World War I, Armenians within the Ottoman Empire attempted to assist

Russian troops in their fight against the Turks. The Turkish government then attempted to deport nearly two million Armenians to Syria and Mesopotamia. Although the numbers are highly disputed, it seems clear that at least 600,000 Armenians—and as many as 2,500,000—died during the massacres or deportations, which has led many to call this episode a "genocide."[17]

Yet it was not only a genocide. Ronald Suny, an historian of Armenia, suggests that along with the threat to the actual physical survival of a people, there can be threats to their cultural survival as a distinct unit. In some ways, he says, "ethnocide," which is the "systematic destruction of a culture," might be even more of a threat to a national or ethnic group than an attempt at genocide.[18] He comments that the Armenians are a people who are "living in permanent danger of assimilation or acculturation—if not annihilation."[19] Indeed, this fear of the loss of cultural identity may be compounded by the reality that the current state of Armenia is much smaller than "historical" Armenia. Mount Ararat, Armenia's most holy mountain, is now in the territory of Turkey (although it is clearly visible from balconies and rooftops in Yerevan), and many Armenians told me that Nakhchivan, the portion of Azerbaijan that is separated from the rest of Azerbaijan by Armenia (see map on page xv), was historically Armenian. This sense of territorial encroachment was a theme in many of the interviews I conducted in Armenia, and indeed it was also a source of justification for the current conflict in Nagorno-Karabakh. We cannot give up Nagorno-Karabakh, people told me, because our identity would be that much more diminished.

We can hear echoes of such fears of cultural or national annihilation in other places, too. In Sri Lanka, the Sinhalese are a majority, and yet they still can feel under threat; one Sinhalese political party has published a letter claiming that the ultimate goal of the LTTE is to rule all of Sri Lanka, with the result that the Sinhalese will suffer the same fate as the majority group in Rwanda, the Hutus (that is, genocide).[20] Tamils have expressed similar fears; one Tamil nationalist publication has argued that the 1983 riots, together with the actions of the Sri Lankan government against the Tamils, should be considered "genocide."[21] And just as in the case of Armenia, historical events in Sri Lanka helped to confirm and intensify such fears. In 1981, Sri Lankan police and security forces burned the main library in the predominantly Tamil town of Jaffna. This library held 95,000 books, including a number of irreplaceable Tamil documents. Stanley Tambiah, a long-time scholar of Sri Lanka, characterized that burning by suggesting that it "has come to signify for many a living Tamil the apogean barbarity of Sinhalese vindictiveness that seeks physical as well as cultural obliteration."[22] Indeed, this event plays a significant role in Tamil Web sites and other publicity materials devoted to the conflict.[23] The destruction of monuments, religious sites, and other symbols of cultural identity can serve as very powerful threats to identity.

The fear of loss of cultural identity does not have to come through experiences of such extreme violence and killing. Quebec is currently a very successful and thriving province of Canada, yet there is evidence that fear of cultural assimilation is a very powerful force there. Perhaps the most dramatic issue is a piece of legislation called "Bill 101—The Charter of the French Language." Bill 101 was enacted in Quebec in 1977. Its goal is to promote the use of French in business and public affairs in Quebec. The *Office de la Langue Francaise* (called by many the "language police") is charged with issuing "francization" certificates to businesses who demonstrate that they have promoted French in their businesses. In recent years this office has been embroiled in controversy when it has attempted to insist that all businesses use French-language computer software, whether or not the employees want to use it.[24] This office has also been the target of a good deal of satire for encouraging "vigilantes" to report violations of the law such as a sign reading "Ploughman's Lunch" outside a pub in Montreal.[25] But there have also been some violent consequences to this principle of promoting the use of French in all businesses. An international chain of coffee shops called "Second Cup" has recently been attacked by firebombs in Montreal because its name is English, not French.[26] Bill 101 does not require companies to change their previously existing trademarks into French, but apparently there are some who believe so strongly in the need to preserve French that they are prepared to use violent means to do so.

The point of all of this is not necessarily a fear that English-speaking Canada is somehow going to destroy Quebecois culture through an explicit and intentional campaign. Quebec is located within a very large Anglo-American culture of English-speaking Canada and the United States. Many in Quebec fear that Quebec's culture could become assimilated into this larger English-speaking milieu if means are not taken now to prevent it. Indeed, a recent poll of Quebecers found that the more they are convinced that the survival of French is at stake in political developments in Canada, the more likely they would be to vote for secession.[27]

Note that I am not suggesting that such fears are groundless. In this case, Quebecers can point to Manitoba, Alberta, and Saskatchewan, all Canadian provinces that in the past had large French-speaking populations and now do not. Francophone culture has essentially disappeared from these places.

The point to be made here is that the fear of psychological annihilation can be as real a fear as of physical annihilation. Even members of a culture as long-standing and vibrant as that of Quebec can feel as though their identity is fragile and under threat. And in some ways, we seem to be primed to feel that threat.

Even simply the way people are characterized can serve as a threat to their identity. It is a commonplace truism among travelers that mistaking an New Zealander for an Australian, or an Estonian for a Russian, can be interpreted as an insult. Whereas such slips are usually inadvertent, language can be used more intentionally to attack the distinctiveness of identity. As noted earlier, Armenians often refer to Azerbaijanis as "Turks," which could be seen as a suggestion that the Azerbaijanis are not a distinct people from their Ottoman relatives. Indeed, a number of Armenian interviewees highlighted to me that because Azerbaijan, as the name of a people, did not exist before the twentieth century, the Azerbaijanis are not really a cohesive people at all. Zori Balayan, an Armenian nationalist and Nagorno-Karabakh supporter, describes the situation more elaborately this way:

> You see, here on the territory of the Russian state, having seized for itself part of historic Armenia, have lived for centuries Armenians, Russians, Persians, Talyshes, Greeks, Tats, Kurds, Caucasian Lezgins and Avars. Later nomadic Turkic tribes arrived. On this ethnic kaleidoscope the Bolsheviks created an artificial "buffer state," as the historians call it, with the aim of building a bridge from Soviet Russia to the East for the "export of revolution." And they called the republic Azerbaijan and all the non-Christians living there Azeri-Turks, or Azerbaijanis.[28]

Balayan lists all the peoples who lived in and near Nagorno-Karabakh and says that none of them are actually "Azerbaijanis," for there are no such people; the term is only a poor creation of the Soviet state. In some ways, this is as direct a threat to identity as an actual physical attack, since it denies to the Azerbaijanis any sense of independent existence.

The conclusion here is that the integrity of our personal and social identities is always potentially at stake. Some social events, such as an explicit or implicit threat from another group, would heighten that sense of fragility. Hence we are likely to be hypersensitive to anything we perceive to be an invasion or incursion upon our identities. Such an incursion might be a physical one, such as when an army invades a territory. It might also be psychological, such as when a group is concerned about its culture and practices being invaded—as people in Quebec feel about the encroachment of Anglo-American culture on their French-speaking society. In a nationalist conflict, when the issues of physical and cultural survival might be raised on both sides, anything that can be perceived as a threat to identity can set off a large response.

Before we can understand the full implications of the nature of identity for nationalism, we have to understand a second way in which identity is under threat. This threat comes from a different source—not the anxiety that comes from believing we are fragile, but the anxiety that comes from believing we are flawed.

Feeling Flawed

There are a number of philosophical, psychological, and religious traditions that suggest that each of us, as individuals, struggles with aspects of our nature that we find unacceptable. The reason we struggle is that we have an ideal image of who we would like to be. When we look at ourselves, however, we find that we do not measure up to this ideal. As a consequence, we feel flawed, sinful, or polluted. Although different traditions conceptualize both the ideal and the "unwanted" aspects of the self in different ways, I would argue that all such concepts attempt to understand a fundamental reality of human nature: that we are worried that we are not what we "should" be. Just as we may feel a threat to our identity from its inherent fragility, we may also feel a threat to our identity from what we fear are its inherent flaws.

The ideal against which we compare ourselves typically comes from popular culture. Society (embodied in religious institutions, schools, and parents) embraces a set of values to which its members are expected to subscribe. In Western society these values might include developing a clearly defined individual identity, a social conscience, confidence, and the desire to do good work. In an Asian society the values might include showing proper respect for ancestors and devoting oneself to the welfare of one's family. In an Islamic society it be might submitting oneself to the will of God and following the commandments of the Koran. All of these social traditions have ways of saying what it means to be a "good" member of society.

However, equally as important is what those social agents say that members of society should *not* feel, or experience, or do. Psychodynamic psychology is one tradition that has considered this question in detail. As I mentioned in chapter 2, the psychodynamic approach asserts that our culture (typically via our parents) tells us that certain feelings or impulses (primarily aggressive and sexual ones) are unacceptable. If we experience such feelings (which we will, because such feelings are a normal part of being human) we will be embarrassed or ashamed by them. Even the idea that such an impulse might arise can cause us anxiety, and we will go to great lengths to ward that anxiety off.[29]

A clinical example, of the sort used in psychodynamic reasoning, might help here. When I worked in a psychiatric hospital, I encountered a young man with a very severe form of obsessive–compulsive disorder. One of his major problems was that he would stand for long periods of time; in one instance he stood in one spot in his apartment, not moving, for three days. His legs swelled up and he became dehydrated, and when his social worker found him like that, she had him hospitalized. This young man was very bright and, in many ways, very charming. During one of our therapy sessions together I asked him what he was doing for those three days while he was standing in his apartment. He replied that he was "thinking." I asked him what he was thinking about. He said that he was remembering a time when he was driving with his mother to a therapy appointment, and the car broke down. They had gotten out of the car, and his mother had asked him to hold the car hood up while she looked inside the engine, which he did. The scene that the young man was imagining while he was standing, however, was what might have happened if he had accidentally dropped the hood while his mother's head was under it. Over and over again, during those three days, that scene came into his thoughts. That is what he was thinking about.

A psychoanalytic interpretation of this event might be that the patient had experienced an impulse that was forbidden—the impulse to drop the hood on his mother's neck. He did not do so, of course, but even the idea that he might want to kill his mother this way was so anxiety-producing that he tried to forget it, to repress it—but it kept coming back, in the form of an obsessive (recurrent and unwanted) thought. The interpretation might go even further and suggest that his compulsive standing could be a way of insuring that he did not carry out that forbidden impulse—because if he did not move, then he could not hurt his mother.

This is an extreme situation, of course, and it is far from certain that this particular thought was the "cause" of the patient's distress. But the point of this example, and indeed of the psychodynamic understanding of human beings, is that we all experience forbidden impulses at one time or another. We all get angry, even at people we love. We all have sexual impulses, sometimes toward those about whom we "shouldn't" feel sexual. Jungian psychoanalysts call this part of us the "shadow"; it is the part of us that is one-sided, limited, sexual, antisocial, and in all manner of ways contrary to "civilized" values.[30] We all have a "shadow"; we all fail to measure up to the ideal of the loving, kind, considerate, compassionate, even-keeled, perfect person that we would so much like to be. The wider the gap between what we think we are and what we want to be, the more we are going to be ashamed of ourselves, the more anxiety we are going to feel, and the more we will try to take steps to rid ourselves of those feelings.

Another approach to therapy in psychology, the humanistic approach, makes similar claims. Abraham Maslow, one of the founding thinkers of this approach to psychology, described it this way:

> The serious thing for each person to recognize vividly and poignantly, each for himself, is that every falling away from species-virtue, every crime against one's own nature, every evil act, *every one without exception records itself* in our unconscious and makes us despise ourselves. . . . If we do something we are ashamed of, it "registers" to our discredit, and if we do something honest or fine or good, it "registers" to our credit. The net results ultimately are either one or the other—either we respect and accept ourselves or we despise ourselves and feel contemptible, worthless, and unlovable. [italics in original][31]

While Maslow broadens the discussion to include not only socially agreed-upon values, but values that are derived intrinsically (from one's own nature), the point is still the same: Making a mistake, acting or even thinking against what we believe to be right leads us to believe that we are bad. The lack of congruence between our evaluation of our own experience and our "ideal" self is very threatening, especially when, as is so often the case, we believe that we are the only ones who are like this. We feel that we are flawed, inadequate, and undeserving, and any experience we have (our actions or our feelings) that confirms this evaluation produces anxiety in us. In fact, this lack of congruence, and our reaction to it, is the cause of many psychological problems. Our constant criticism of our own personality can break down the very identity that we want to preserve.[32]

Feeling Sinful

And in fact, as some writers have pointed out,[33] the Judeo-Christian concept of original or hereditary sin reflects this very same idea. In its most superficial formulation, original sin is the mark or "stain" left upon all of us by Adam's disobeying God when he ate the fruit of the tree of knowledge of good and evil.[34] Each person carries the burden of that sin from birth, simply by virtue of being human. This view is also supported by a section in the Apostle Paul's letter to the Romans, in which he comments:

> Therefore as sin came into the world through one man and death through sin, and so death spread to all men because all men sinned.[35]

Therefore one way of thinking about original sin is that each human being is inescapably tarnished because of Adam's actions. Other theologians have explained this concept by suggesting that we are born *into* a sinful society and participate in it.[36] Either way, this theological concept reflects the same psychological reality: that we believe there is something wrong with us that derives from our actions and also, perhaps, from the very fact of our being human. Feeling flawed is inescapable. In fact, the more we perceive the divine, the more we realize how far we are from it, and the resulting sense of estrangement from God is essentially what we understand as "sin."[37] Paul describes this in very personal terms by saying:

> I do not do the good I want, but the evil I do not want is what I do. Now if I do what I do not want, it is no longer I that do it, but sin that dwells within me. [38]

Paul's description carries with it a sense that the "sin" within us is not "really" us—it is somehow a part of us, yet feels alien. This is a very good description of the similar sense of a rejected part of ourselves that is described in the psychodynamic tradition. We know we have an aspect of ourselves that does evil, that breaks God's laws, that is impure—and that is always there, and a threat to us. By virtue of being human, we have aspects of ourselves that are unacceptable. And yet we cannot escape that sense of being flawed, because it is a part of being human.

I would argue that this idea would not be so popular in Western culture (and more broadly, given the success of Christianity in many societies around the world) if it did not resonate deeply with actual human experience. Even if "original sin" is not a literal theological truth, the basic sense that something is rotten at our core must in some ways be a *psychological* truth. Even in religions in which there is no concept of original sin, there are still indications of this experience. In Islam, there is no doctrine of "original sin" as such; even though the story of Adam and Eve is a part of the Islamic tradition, the Koran holds that God forgave Adam for that disobedience, and hence there is no mark of hereditary sin on humans. In this tradition, humans are, in contrast, born with dignity. The problem is that they are born into a world in which rebellion against authority is the norm, and therefore they must learn to submit to God. So while there is no concept of original sin in Islam, there is a sense that humans are constantly doing the wrong thing—disobeying God. Hinduism also acknowledges sin, in the sense of a violation of moral laws.[39]

In fact, we might say that all of the world's traditions that rely on a dualism of light and dark, heaven and hell, good and evil, or spirit and flesh are in some ways reinforcing these same ideas. Such diverse religious traditions as Judaism, Christianity, Islam, Hinduism, Buddhism, and Zoroastrianism imply that individual human beings must struggle with sin or evil and then try to find ways to extricate themselves from the lure of badness. At the root of all these traditions is the same conception—that somewhere inside us is either the actuality or the propensity to do wrong, and that whatever it is, that propensity is alien to us, something that really should not be there.

Thus we feel haunted by the gnawing suspicion that we are always at risk of giving in to that badness and thereby having our identity corrupted or destroyed. This worry can have a substantial effect on our sense of self— after all, if we are really so bad inside, why would anyone think we were good at all?

Feeling Defiled or Polluted

Another way in which we can experience feelings of not measuring up is to feel that there is something defiled or dirty about us. Over and over again, religious traditions prescribe purification rituals to help people shed that sense of defilement and to bring them closer to God. Psychologically, the feeling of being defiled is very much the same as the feeling that we do not measure up to an ideal; either way, we feel as though part of us is not what it should be.

There is a whole range of beliefs and practices that illustrate these concerns regarding pollution and purity. Some pollution is perceived as the result of contact with objects or people who are seen as ritually impure. In the Hebrew Bible, for example, the books of Leviticus and Deuteronomy provide many examples of what is clean and what is unclean. Some animals, such as the ox, sheep, goat, gazelle, antelope, and mountain sheep, are said to be fit for eating. However, the camel, the hare, the rock badger, and swine are unclean and not to be eaten, nor their carcasses touched.[40] In Hinduism, members of high castes must not have any physical contact with

Untouchables, who are members of a caste that carries out societal functions that are seen as impure. If, for example, a Brahmin (a high-caste) person touches a piece of bamboo or a rope at the same time as an Untouchable does, the Brahmin is considered to be severely polluted. The same is true if the Brahmin steps on a straw-covered floor at the same time as an Untouchable. The straw is believed to transmit the pollution from the one to the other.[41] Other kinds of pollution come from natural bodily processes. In Islam, the faithful must perform a ritual bath anytime they have entered a state of ritual impurity called *janabat. Janabat* is entered if a man or woman has had sexual intercourse, or if a man has excreted semen, voluntarily or involuntarily. Until the person has performed the bath, he or she may not touch a Koran or recite several of the holy verses from it.[42]

One argument that has been made about such rituals is that they are based on rational concerns about hygiene. In some cases, that may well be the case. But it does not have to be so. As Mary Douglas, one of the most prominent investigators of purity and pollution, has noted, the notion of pollution is relative. In one example she gives, a visiting holy woman came to an Indian village and was purified by water mixed with cow dung. The rationale was that since cows are sacred, even cow dung is more pure than any human being.[43] Concerns about ritual purity are about how we *feel,* not about how literally clean we are.

It is worth noting here that just as in the psychodynamic conception of the "unwanted" aspects of the self, the target of pollution concerns often has to do with sexuality. Sexual feelings, various kinds of sexual activity, or even sexual activity itself are often seen as polluting or potentially dangerous. As I noted in chapter 1, outgroup devaluation often contains the sentiment that "we" are more pure and more moral than "they" are; thus accusations of the sexual immorality of the "other," such as the accusations I repeated about Armenians sexually violating Azerbaijani women, are common. Indeed, wartime rumors and propaganda very commonly focus on the sexual atrocities, including sexual mutilations and rape, committed by the enemy.[44] Unfortunately, those atrocities are not just rumors and propaganda. Combatants commonly commit sexual violence against women in wartime, including periods nationalist and ethnic conflict. In recent years men have raped or sexually assaulted women on a broad scale during the conflicts in Bosnia,[45] Liberia,[46] Algeria,[47] Rwanda[48], and many others. There is increasing evidence that, at least in some cases, these attacks are part of a deliberate strategy to demoralize the enemy. In the war in the Balkans in the early 1990s, for example, when mass rape was used against

Muslim women, one explanation was that the Serbs were consciously attempting to pollute Muslim identity—first by sexually violating Muslim women, and second by producing children that were of mixed heritage, thereby contaminating the racial purity of the Muslims.[49]

There are a variety of potential dynamics underlying sexual atrocities and mass rape, such as a reaction to strict societal control over sexuality[50] or sexual violence as a way for men to show solidarity with each other or to prove their "manhood." The point, however, is that we as humans often have a difficult relationship with sexuality, and thus sexuality, in turn, ends up being one of the battlegrounds in which nationalist conflicts are fought.

Cleansing and Purging

Our natural reaction to feeling dirty is to cleanse ourselves, and this tendency is seen in nationalist conflict in very vivid terms. Ernest Becker describes the connection between conflict and a feeling of pollution this way:

> The irony is that men are always dissatisfied and guilty in small and large ways, and this is what drives them to a search for purity where all dissatisfaction can come to a head and be wiped away. Men try to qualify for eternalization by being clean and by cleansing the world around them of the evil, the dirty. . . . The highest heroism is the stamping out of those who are tainted.[51]

Becker's point is that we escape our fear of death by trying to become perfect and getting rid of those people who remind us of our inherent imperfection. Rhetoric about ridding society of those who are evil or bad, is of course, a persistent feature of religious and secular conflict. In Pakistan, for example, the leader of a guerrilla group called "The Army of the Pure" says that his group is obligated to "destroy the forces of evil and disbelief," and trains young men to fight against India in Kashmir.[52] When the Khmer Rouge came to power in Cambodia in April 1975, they began a process in which they attempted to remake Cambodian society by removing all those who did not support the new political ideology.[53] They evacuated Phnom Penh and targeted certain classes of people, such as military officers, teachers, doctors, and intellectuals, for harassment and execution. Approximately two million people eventually died from starvation or were killed during this period of time, at least partly through a desire on the part of the radicals (and supported by some of the population) to create a "pure" new society. The attempts to cleanse the Communist party in Stalin's Soviet Union in the 1930s were called "purges," and they resulted in millions of deaths.[54] In addition to drives to achieve political purity, there are drives to achieve racial purity. One influential book at the turn of the century argued that the white race was in danger of being destroyed by intermarriage with nonwhite groups (which included Asians, Jews, Southern Europeans, and Eastern Europeans), and advocated identifying the least desirable ten percent of humanity and preventing them from reproducing.[55] Nazi Germany promoted the view that Jews were impure and would destroy the German race. Many neo-Nazi and white supremacist groups today make a similar argument. Attempts to purify ourselves by wiping out others are widespread.

Of course, the most prominent use of the concept of purity and pollution is in the term "ethnic cleansing," which is so often used to describe campaigns of mass population shifts. Attempts by majority groups to drive minority ethnic groups out of their homes has been well documented in the Balkans.[56] Sinhalese, Tamils, Armenians, Azerbaijanis, Palestinians, Tutsis, Hutus, and many other national groups around the world have experienced, to varying degrees, attempts to create ethnically "pure" villages, regions, or homelands. And the methods that have been used in these instances have at times been quite brutal, from forced evacuations to mass rapes to executions.

The ferocity of ethnic cleansing around the world suggests that just as individuals try to rid themselves of those aspects of themselves that they find bad, evil, or dirty, national groups do the same with individuals from rival groups. And the function may well be the same: If the people who are seen as "unclean" are allowed to remain, the integrity of the national group, in the sense of its soundness and health, is called into question. The concept of pollution is another way of expressing the inherent unease we have with our own sense of identity.

Conclusions

In essence, we as humans easily feel threatened. We want to believe that our identity is solid, and yet we suspect that it is fragile. We want to believe that we are good and moral, but we suspect that we are not. We are afraid of various aspects of ourselves, and so we reject them and see them as alien, as sin or pollution. We are not who we want to be.

The result of all this is that we feel flawed, inadequate, or unfulfilled, and we do not want to feel that way. We crave a sense of being good, being just, and being right, but we do not know how to get it. However, nationalism provides us with a way out of this situation. Nationalism provides a way for us to join together with others, to be convinced that we are good, and to live in the service of a just cause. How nationalism meets our need to feel justified is the subject of the next chapter.

Chapter 5

NATIONALISM AND HUMAN NEEDS

As humans, we have to contend with a variety of threats to our identity, from the gradual deterioration of our physical bodies to attacks on our cultural integrity from others. In addition, we have to cope with the reality that we cannot always measure up to the standards that we have set for ourselves. Underlying our sense of self is a creeping suspicion that we are not as good as we should be. Nationalism provides us with a way to deal with this reality. It gives us the opportunity to feel moral, right, and just. It gives us a way to join with others in a heroic struggle. It gives a sense of purpose and meaning to our lives, and even to our deaths. Nationalism meets a variety of very important human needs. How it does so is the topic of this chapter.

Our Cause Is Just

First and foremost, nationalism provides us with a way of feeling that we are right. Feeling right is a very powerful motivator. Think of the last time you were in an interpersonal conflict, such as a disagreement with a spouse or co-worker. If you really believed that you were right, how likely was it that you would give up your claims and give in to what the other person wanted? Even when being in a conflict is painful, and even if you have a strong relationship with the person you are arguing with, the feeling of being right is very hard to give up. Being right fills some of the deep voids in our identity that I discussed in the last chapter. It helps us feel justified and worthwhile. Being right is so powerful, in fact, that at times we would rather maintain that sense of rightness by staying in the conflict than to risk losing it by giving the conflict up.

Let me give some examples. Nationalist groups commonly assert that their cause is just. In the Armenia-Azerbaijan conflict, the Armenian side says that Nagorno-Karabakh should belong to them, and always has. First, the argument goes, Nagorno-Karabakh has been populated by Armenians for three thousand years.[1] A variety of invaders, including Russians, Tatars, and Turks, have wanted to possess Artsakh (the Armenian name for Nagorno-Karabakh) but no one ever captured Karabakh because the Karabakh people are very strong and able to protect it.[2] Second, the Karabakh Armenians have long been oppressed. During the Soviet period, Armenian children were given only two Armenian language lessons a week, as compared to Azerbaijani language lessons every day, even in Armenian-language schools; and in 1987, teaching Armenian history was even made illegal in Nagorno-Karabakh schools.[3] Later, at the beginning of the armed conflict, Azerbaijanis committed atrocities against Karabakh Armenians as well as Armenians in Sumgait and Baku. In the Armenian view, therefore, justice demands that Armenians be compensated for these events.

And most importantly, Armenian control over Nagorno-Karabakh would right historical wrongs. Historically, Armenia was much larger than it is now, and because Nagorno-Karabakh is part of that "historical Armenia" it is only right that Armenians claim what was originally theirs. Plus, returning Nagorno-Karabakh to Armenian control would redress the 1915 genocide.[4] The Turks attempted to annihilate the Armenians then, and the Azerbaijanis are trying to do it now. (Even though the Azerbaijanis are not the same Turks who committed that massacre, they are related.) Such aggression cannot be allowed to stand; Armenians must be able to defend themselves. For all these reasons, this argument goes, the cause of the Karabakh Armenians is just.

Zori Balayan, one of the founders of the Karabakh movement, summarizes his view of the justice of the Karabakh cause by writing:

> The Karabakh movement as a living being is reminiscent of Moses, for whom God was justice incarnate. For this reason, God forbid that anybody should perceive as merely a wish to preach my attempts to draw a parallel with the difficult history of a people which was liberated from slavery by obedience to moral laws. . . . I have never seen the words "Thou shalt not kill" written by God's hand as an encouragement to leave murderers unpunished . . . Could justice calmly watch the life of a whole people being made "bitter with hard bondage . . ."? And say in these circumstances, for exam-

ple, "love your neighbor!" Could justice calmly listen as pharaoh "charged all
his people, saying, every son that is born ye shall cast into the river . . ."? . . .
Surely God understood that his commandments were worth nothing if evil
was not punished.[5]

Balayan uses biblical imagery to evoke feelings of justice and righteousness. The Karabakh movement is Moses, the leader that brings all Armenians—not just those living in Karabakh—into freedom. The conclusion to this
argument is that Armenians should fight for Nagorno-Karabakh because it is
the right thing to do, even at the potential cost of comfort, property, and lives.

However, if you were to ask Azerbaijanis about the right to rule
Nagorno-Karabakh, they would likely tell you that Nagorno-Karabakh has
long been populated by Azerbaijanis, not Armenians.[6] They would say that
Armenians are relative newcomers to the area, having been brought to the
area by Russia to displace local Azerbaijanis and serve as a tool of Russia's
policy to expand its control south toward the Persian Gulf[7] and to create a
buffer zone against the Muslim peoples to the south.[8] Indeed, an impressive
new line of scholarship on the history of the area is demonstrating the
long-standing Azerbaijani claim to this land.[9] In addition, the Azerbaijanis
say, there are other, more moral reasons that Azerbaijan should control
Nagorno-Karabakh. The Azerbaijani population has suffered tremendously
at the hands of the Armenians. In 1988, Armenia expelled 160,000 Azerbaijanis who had lived in the republic of Armenia for generations. Those
refugees are still sitting in refugee camps around Azerbaijan, living in grim
conditions with virtually no hope for the future.[10] Then in February 1992,
Armenian soldiers massacred hundreds of innocent Azerbaijani civilians in
an attack on Khojaly, not far from the Nagorno-Karabakh capital of
Stepanakert.[11] And most importantly, ethnic Armenian troops have pushed
all Azerbaijani residents out of Nagorno-Karabakh and a number of surrounding provinces, depriving those people of their homes and land while
adding to the refugee problem in Azerbaijan. If ethnic Armenian troops are
occupying 20 percent of Azerbaijan, this argument goes, the only justice,
under international law, would be for Azerbaijan to receive those lands back.

Vafa Guluzade, a governmental figure in Azerbaijan, succinctly summarizes an Azerbaijani position on the conflict:

> It might be noted that even the Nazis allowed inhabitants of their occupied
> territories to stay and live there. But Armenians have rid Azerbaijanis
> from the entire occupied territories. Khojaly, a small Azerbaijani town in
> Nagorno-Karabakh, is a sad example of genocide, when overnight the

whole town was destroyed, more than 700 innocent civilians, including many women and children, were murdered and others were forcefully deported.[12]

Guluzade compares the Armenians to the Nazis and suggests that the Armenians are even worse. Justice, in his view, is clearly on the side of the Azerbaijanis. So both sides in this conflict believe that their cause is just, and they can give a variety of arguments to say why. Indeed, similar arguments about the historical wrongs that must be righted can be found in appeals on behalf of the LTTE,[13] Tibet,[14] Abkhazia,[15] Quebec,[16] and others.

Of course, such statements need to be considered in context; they are often oriented toward the international community and are designed to win support for the cause of those who make them. But I would argue that these arguments are not simply propaganda. They also serve a purpose for those who are directly involved in the conflict, giving them a sense of justification. Arguments about justice have a great deal of power on a personal and emotional level. If you have ever been in a serious conflict with someone, then you may have a sense of what truly righteous anger is like. It is a stomach-churning experience. On the one hand, there is often great frustration at feeling victimized, betrayed, hurt, or ignored, depending on what the situation is. And yet, there is also a satisfying aspect to righteous anger. It helps us to obtain clarity from the complicated tangle of our feelings. When someone has clearly done us wrong, we do not have to apologize or feel guilty about the rage and bitterness that we feel. It is our right, as the aggrieved party, to feel those feelings and express them, and no one can fault us for it. We get sympathy from others. And we feel fully justified, in a way that few other life situations allow us to feel.

Imagine a situation in which a husband has ambivalent feelings about his wife. He is angry at her and is unsure whether or not he really wants to be married to her. However, he does not really want to express those feelings because he feels guilty about them—after all, they are married, and he promised to stay with her. Then his wife cheats on him, sleeping with another man. The husband loses in that situation because he feels hurt and betrayed. And yet he also gains something, because he now has a sense of moral authority—being the one who was hurt, he can be angry, and he can act out his feelings without criticism. If he then did his own betraying and went out with another woman, he might well be able to justify that to himself as a way of evening the score. His being betrayed is a significant blow, but his being wronged brings with it opportunities to stabilize his own sense of self by giving him license to feel and express what he already was experiencing. In fact, difficult as it is for him to accept the painful feelings of being betrayed, we might well expect him to cling to them because of the sense of righteousness they bring him.

And in a situation of real nationalist conflict, when property, territory, and lives are at stake, all of these feelings will be intensified. Zori Balayan describes a funeral for an Armenian soldier during the Karabakh war, in which the dead man's five-year-old son stood next to the coffin stroking his father's hair as though the father might soon wake up from his sleep.[17] It is easy to imagine the grief and fury that we might feel if we were in that situation. There would be the devastating grief and emptiness of losing a loved one. And we would certainly feel hostility toward the Azerbaijanis who killed him. But there might also be other feelings too, feelings that we probably would not talk about. We might question whether the sacrifice was really worth it. We might feel anger at those on our side who did not protect this soldier in the battle. We might even be angry at the soldier himself for putting himself in danger and abandoning us in this way. Enduring such a conflicting welter of feelings would be difficult for anyone. A natural way to deal with this confusion would be to direct all of our feelings outward, in a wave of righteous anger against the enemy. We can blame the enemy for everything and not deal with our own role in starting or maintaining the conflict. It is natural to feel anger after a very real tragedy such as this one. But it is also easier to focus and act on the anger than to acknowledge the potentially disturbing feelings of our own responsibility in the situation.

Victimhood

Feeling that our cause is just can be powerful, because much of life is filled with ambiguities. In a nationalist movement in which there is a clear enemy, these emotional and moral ambiguities fade, and the sense of good and bad emerges much more sharply. We can feel good about our group and despise the enemy without any ambiguity or guilt. We can feel like knights, avenging evil and slaying dragons.[18] Even our tragedies can become badges of honor, as we continue the struggle despite the hardships and costs. Indeed, one powerful way in which individuals can achieve a feeling of being right is to have been victimized, and to have others recognize that victimization. One would think that in a group's stories about its own history, national triumphs might play the dominant role. However, national *tragedies* often play an even more prominent role in the way that a nation sees itself.[19]

For example, "Black January" is a national tragedy for the Azerbaijani people. On January 20, 1990, Soviet troops entered Baku, ostensibly to protect the Armenian population there. (Most of Baku's substantial Armenian population had fled or been evacuated from Baku several days earlier after anti-Armenian rioting.) Instead of protecting anyone, the Soviet troops killed at least 130 Azerbaijanis and wounded many more.[20] This event is now memorialized in "Martyr's Lane," an area on a hill on the south side of Baku. A long lane is flanked on each side by gravestones bearing the names, birthdates, and pictures of each of the Azerbaijanis killed on that day. The Azerbaijan government has subsequently added graves on each side of the lane for those who were killed in the war over Nagorno-Karabakh. At the end of the lane, on the site of a former Soviet monument, an eternal flame burns. Yerevan, the capital of Armenia, features a similar monument. It stands atop a hill with a commanding view of the city and is accompanied by a museum honoring the genocide of 1915. It too features an eternal flame, surrounded by obelisks that represent the various regions in which Armenians have traditionally lived. It is accompanied by a museum dedicated to honoring the victims of the massacres.

These events have become part of these people's collective memories; they were mentioned in nearly all of the interviews I conducted with people in Armenia and Azerbaijan, and they help set the context for their understanding of the current conflict.[21] Most national groups have similar historical traumas, such as the Holocaust for the Jews, Pearl Harbor for the Americans, and the defeat at the Battle of Kosovo in 1389 for the Serbs. These were experiences of defeat, and yet they have become rallying points, times that are remembered in speeches, rallies, and memorials. Public acknowledgement of these tragedies allows people to grieve for the losses that their groups have endured, much as a cemetery headstone does for individuals who have lost family members.[22]

And yet, such reminders serve other psychological functions too. The memory of such events is kept alive because it also confers upon the aggrieved people the status of victimhood. After all, being a victim brings with it a number of benefits. Being a victim of another's aggression means that we have suffered unjustly. Being a victim confers upon us a kind of moral authority—a sense that we *deserve* to be treated specially. In fact, being a victim is so powerful that we would expect people to assume victim status if they can. And indeed, we can find many national groups invoking victim status,[23] including such unlikely candidates as present-day China.[24] Being a victim gives us the right to take action against our enemies while blaming them for the violence at the same time.

Obviously, crucial to this justification process is having others accept the group's victim status, and that is why we see so much effort on the part of national groups to gain acknowledgement of their trauma. Armenian organizations have worked to make recognition of the genocide of 1915 widespread, with a good deal of success. Governmental bodies in Argentina, Russia, Canada, Greece, the United States, Lebanon, Belgium, France, Sweden, and Uruguay have passed resolutions acknowledging the genocide, as have a number of towns and cities in France, Italy, and the United States.[25] The Azerbaijanis, in turn, also publicize their tragedies.[26] Tamil nationalist Web sites—both the official site of the LTTE in London and other sites, primarily housed in Canada—emphasize the legitimacy of the LTTE's armed struggle, and document in great detail the atrocities that they say have been committed against Tamils by the Sri Lankan armed forces.[27] Sinhalese nationalist publications and Web sites similarly highlight atrocities that they claim Tamils, and particularly the LTTE, have committed against innocent Sinhalese.[28]

Obviously, as in the discussion above, these kinds of arguments are political acts, aimed toward generating sympathy for the nationalists' cause. But that is precisely the point. Attaining an acknowledged victim status gives a people a moral legitimacy to continue its struggle, and such status can play an important role in the justness of the cause. At the same time, victimhood certainly fuels the flames of nationalist conflict. One way in which it does so is to make a group less likely to acknowledge the victimization of others. John Mack, a psychiatrist, was involved in a number of workshops and discussions between Israelis, Egyptians, and Palestinians in the 1970s. His observation from these discussions was that those present were often so focused on expressing the historical traumas their own peoples had undergone that they simply did not hear the descriptions of the other group's pain. The other group, in turn, then interpreted that lack of attention as a *denial* of their trauma, and the relationship between the participants correspondingly worsened.[29] Mack has termed this "the egoism of victimization,"[30] and sees overcoming it to be one of the major tasks in establishing communication between conflicting groups.

In many nationalist conflicts, however, there are even more powerful motivators for not acknowledging the victimhood of the other group. If one group acknowledges that the other group has a claim to victimhood, then the first group loses its moral advantage over the other. Politically, this acknowledgement would take away from the justification for military action or other strategic issues. And psychologically, it would take away the sense of moral justification that we seek so strongly. Hence there are powerful psychological factors that would militate *against* our acknowledging the victim status of a national group that we are in conflict with. And thus negotiations become much more difficult, and it becomes much easier to be locked into a cycle of waiting until the other group has sufficiently accepted the rightness of "our" position.

Interestingly, while our own victimhood might hinder our recognition of the suffering of an "enemy," our striving for justification does not stop us from acknowledging the victim status of other groups that we perceive are like us, so that their victimization can bolster our legitimacy too. For example, during the NATO bombing of Kosovo in 1998, a Tamil organization in the United States produced a series of materials that made a direct comparison between the situation of the Tamils in their struggle for independence, and the struggle of the Kosovo Albanians for their independence.[31] The materials highlight that: Kosovo contains one fifth the landmass of Serbia, while Tamil Eelam contains one third the landmass of Sri Lanka. Albanians constitute 90 percent of the population in Kosovo, while Tamils constitute 99 percent of the population in the northern province of Sri Lanka. The Kosovo Albanians were being dominated by an army that consisted entirely of Serbs; while the Sri Lankan Tamils are now being dominated by an army that consists entirely of Sinhalese. The list of comparisons goes on. If NATO felt so strongly about rescuing Albanians in Kosovo from the Serbs, these materials say, why should they not also rescue Tamils in Sri Lanka from the Sinhalese? There are other examples of the members of one group allying themselves in some way with victims of another time or another tragedy. Most obvious is the way in which some have used the term "holocaust" to describe attacks against their own people, thereby inviting comparisons to the Nazi genocide of the Jews.[32]

Thus we are reluctant to acknowledge the victimhood of our opponents during a nationalist conflict, while we will insist that they recognize ours. We want to promote our own victimization and deny that of our opponents because victimhood confers power. For us as individuals, it provides a sense of rightness and moral solidity that can help counteract the natural feelings of being flawed that we carry with us. For us as a nation, victim status helps us to gain sympathy and aid from others while bolstering our public cause for the military or other activities that we are carrying out in service of our movement. It is easy to see why nations would highlight their historical tragedies and traumas.

Retribution and Revenge

One of the consequences of emphasizing our victimhood is that it leads us to retribution and revenge. In an abstract sense, retribution is an attempt to set the scales of justice right again. If we have suffered a historical wrong, then it is just to have it righted. If our territory has been taken, we deserve to have it back. But unfortunately, nationalist conflict has more dimensions than that. Injuries that one nation inflicts upon another are not simply questions of resources stolen or territory that can be returned. Historical grievances have a psychological component that makes the desire for revenge very common.

Here is an example at the individual level. Let's say I am walking down the street. Someone comes running up to me, pushes me over, grabs my briefcase out of my hand, and runs away. I have now been victimized. There are two components to my injury. The first is the actual injury itself, which is the loss of my briefcase (as well as the bruises I might have obtained when I fell over). But the second aspect is that by pushing me over and taking my briefcase, the aggressor has conveyed a sense of *disrespect* for me. The aggressor must have believed that I have fewer rights than he has or that I am less important, or that I deserve this kind of treatment for some reason. So being injured has both physical and psychological aspects. Correspondingly, redressing the injury also would have two aspects (assuming the mugger was caught). One would be getting compensated for the actual injury—receiving my briefcase back, and perhaps getting medical costs paid. That would be restitution. Restitution, however, does not address the psychological injury that I have sustained due to the mugger's lack of respect for me.

That is the point of revenge. Revenge seeks to right not the physical aspects of the injury, but the psychological ones; it addresses the *relationship* between the aggressor and the aggrieved, preferably by changing the aggressor's *evaluation* of the aggrieved. I want the mugger to recognize that he is not better than me and does not have the right to push me down just because he wants to. Fritz Heider, a social psychologist, makes this point by noting that in everyday language we tend to use expressions such as "I'll teach him a lesson!" and "He has to learn that he can't do that!"—which suggest that the psychological purpose of retribution is to change the way that the aggressor thinks.[33]

Because we evaluate ourselves partially by how others think of us, and because there is such a large component of disrespect in being injured, retribution after an injury can seem to be not just desirable, but imperative. This is often put in terms of the necessity to "save face" or "restore pride," or to "avenge the honor" of an individual or a people. For example, in Armenia I was told many times that the Nagorno-Karabakh conflict meant the time had finally come for Armenians to "stand up" for themselves and not take being trampled on anymore; the military success of the Karabakh forces would show the "Turks" (that is, both the Turks and the Azerbaijanis) that they could not push the Armenians around anymore. "Honor" and "pride" are, essentially, synonyms for how we evaluate ourselves and how we think others evaluate us. Restoring one's honor is simply changing what the aggressor feels about us, so that we, in turn, might feel better about ourselves. So when people feel aggrieved, either for a personal injury or for an injury done to their nation, they are likely to want to have some kind of retribution, as a way of protecting the integrity of their identity.

And we can see cycles of retribution in many nationalist conflicts. The attacks on Armenians in Sumgait in 1988 were said to be in response to the killings of two Azerbaijani youths in Agdam, in Nagorno-Karabakh, several days earlier. The 1983 riots against Tamils in Colombo were said to be in response to the killings of 13 Sri Lankan soldiers in Jaffna. The killings of the soldiers in Jaffna, in turn, might well have been in retaliation for army atrocities against Tamil civilians, such as the allegation that soldiers had raped a number of female Tamil students.[34] The parties in such tense situations usually trade accusations and counteraccusations about who is responding to whom. And as we know from the discussion in chapter 1, reliable information can be difficult to obtain, and rumors, particularly of atrocities committed by the enemy, flow quickly and easily. Thus cycles of revenge and retribution can develop easily as people, fueled by the desire to achieve justice and proper respect for themselves and their national group, attempt to "even the score" with those they perceive as aggressors.

The problem with retribution, of course, is that it tends to escalate.[35] There are several reasons for this. First, while "an eye for an eye" might sound like a prescription for retribution that maintains the equity of harm done to each party, in practice it is not psychologically satisfying. Instead, as the classical avenger Atreus says in Seneca's play *Thyestes,* "Great crimes you don't avenge, unless you outdo them."[36] When the grandfather of the Carthaginian general Hannibal was killed, Hannibal is said to have taken revenge by capturing an entire city and killing the 3,000 male captives at the spot where his grandfather died.[37] More recently, after a bomb attack on a school bus killed two Israeli teachers and wounded five Israeli children in the Gaza Strip, Israel responded by shooting rockets into Gaza City and a refugee camp, wounding 62 people.[38] We can see the psychological motivation behind escalating a vengeful act; we want the other to be taught a lesson, and so we want that lesson to be very vivid and clear. The act that then comes in response to the retribution might be similarly strong, and the cycle of retribution would continue.

In fact, even if the act of revenge is not an escalation, there is psychological research that suggests that it will be perceived as such; retributive acts are nearly always considered more serious by the one who receives them than by those who perform them.[39] Again, if we conceive of retribution as an act that protects the self, and being injured as experiencing a disregard for the self coming from the other party, then this makes sense. We feel injured not only by the extent to which we actually lose something; we feel injured according to how much the other person or group devalues us. If someone takes revenge against us, then we understand that they did not think we had the right to do the original action we took against them; and then we feel the need to uphold our honor, our pride, and our self-esteem against them again. Revenge also works in the opposite way. If we experience an injury to our people, and we decide *not* to respond or take revenge, we might be accused of not being sufficiently patriotic or nationalist. One woman I met in Baku told me of her recent realization that perhaps the Armenians were not as bad as she had always thought. However, she was concerned that if she gave up her hatred for them, this might be tantamount to giving up her love for her own people. In this sense, holding a desire to seek revenge can be a defense of one's own people; giving it up would be letting go of one's respect for oneself.

The point of all this is that just as righteous anger serves our psychological needs, entering into a cycle of revenge and retribution does too. Our need for vengeance goes beyond the actual hurts that have been done to us; it also stems from our own dissatisfaction with ourselves. As Nietzsche put it, "Whoever is dissatisfied with himself is always ready to revenge himself therefore; we others will be his victims."[40] Finding refuge in victimization and anger helps us, even if temporarily, to deal with the anxiety of tolerating who we really are.

Finding Meaning in Life

Finally, nationalism helps us find a sense of meaning in life. Many writers have noted that having a purpose for living is a central part of being human. Erich Fromm argued that we all have a need for a "frame of orientation and devotion," some kind of psychological "map" that not only tells us where we stand in relation to society and to the world, but that also provides a goal for our action.[41] Of the nature of this devotion, Fromm commented:

> The objects of man's devotion vary. He can be devoted to an idol which requires him to kill his children or to an ideal that makes him protect children; he can be devoted to the growth of life or to its destruction. . . . He can be devoted to the most diverse goals and idols; yet while the differences in the objects of devotion are of immense importance, the need for devotion itself is a primary, existential need demanding fulfillment regardless of *how* this need is fulfilled.[42]

Fromm's point is not that all goals are equally valid; it is simply that we all need to have some kind of goal or system of values that helps us understand our place in life. As Fromm noted, people find vastly different ways of bringing meaning to their lives. And yet, having a clear frame of reference or set of values is not simply a given. The search for a viable set of enduring values is, after all, essentially the definition of "identity crisis," as the term is understood in Western psychology.[43] Not having a clear set of values or goals makes us feel as though we are adrift and incomplete.

While we all must find a sense of meaning and value in our lives, the social and historical context can make the search for meaning more difficult. Rapid social change can force people to adapt to unfamiliar social roles and can leave them feeling anxious,[44] and can make a society more prone to mass violence.[45] Large-scale social changes also intensify people's search for their own identity and history.[46] And some have suggested that the collapse of the Soviet Union provided just such a vacuum of meaning for the people of the former Soviet Union and Eastern Europe, who thus had to search for other "frames of devotion" (in Fromm's term), particularly nationalism, to find purpose for their lives.[47] Nationalism does in fact help to fill the void left when social disruption occurs. If I am part of a nationalist movement, what I do in that movement is important, because it relates both to the history of my people and to their future; therefore the meaning of my life extends beyond just me. Even if I were to die in the conflict, my death would have meaning because it would be in the service of a goal.

In Stepanakert, the capital of Nagorno-Karabakh, I met a family that lost a son, Arman,[48] in the conflict. Arman grew up learning about Armenian history from his parents, an Armenian language teacher and a history teacher. He early on became involved in the nationalist cause, circulating petitions, organizing, and eventually procuring weapons for the Nagorno-Karabakh forces. When the conflict began in earnest, he joined the armed forces. At the battle for Shusha, an Azerbaijani-populated town in the hills above Stepanakert, Arman helped a number of members of his unit escape an Azerbaijani attack by laying down covering fire for them. Afterward, finding himself surrounded, he blew himself up with a hand grenade. He was 19 years old.

Arman's parents were understandably distraught over the loss of their son and feel the pain of this loss even several years later. However, they emphasized to me over and over again that his death brought honor to his family and to all of the people of Nagorno-Karabakh, and that it was not in vain. He has been memorialized on Armenian television and awarded several posthumous medals. He has been written about in the Armenian diaspora press. In these ways he has inspired others for the cause. Of course, one could explain such a sentiment by claiming that his parents are simply trying to rationalize away a tragedy. But it is not simply that. Arman knew about the danger *before* he joined up, but he already believed that the cause was more important than life. People engage in conflict knowing that they may well be injured or die. But dying in the service of an important cause can be something positive, a goal to achieve. Indeed, dying in the cause of a nationalist struggle can even bring a kind of immortality, as those who have fallen are often immortalized in sculptures, songs, or martyrs' holidays. So engaging in a nationalist conflict may bring meaning not only to life, but also to death.

Conflict May Be Preferable to Peace

If we are convinced that our cause is just, then sacrifice in the service of the cause is right. Fighting on in the face of heavy losses is right. Refusing to resolve a conflict until justice (as we understand it) has prevailed is right. Unfortunately, because being right is so attractive to us, both sides in nationalist conflicts tend to feel that their cause is just. Atrocities and deaths happen on both sides, and so each side has good reason to persevere, and good reason to seek revenge on the other side. Historical inequities live on as part of national narratives and identities, and continue to play a role in the present. And feeling victimized provides us with such a feeling of justice and rightness that it is hard to let go of it. Giving up victim status means giving up the moral right to get what we want. Forgiving the other side for the actions they have committed in the conflict means giving up our right to revenge. The payoffs for clinging to conflict are strong; we do not have to tolerate those feelings and those people who are upsetting to us. And the losses in ending a conflict are substantial—we lose that sense of rightness and moral justification that is such a precious commodity for us. It is easy to see why nationalist conflicts are so tenacious.

The conclusion of this line of thinking is that for many people, conflict may be preferable to peace. Long-standing nationalist conflicts have devastating effects on many of the very people who are involved in them. And yet the conflicts continue because conflicts help us bring meaning to our lives, bring certainty to ambiguous situations, stabilize our sense of identity, and provide us with a sense of being just and right. It makes sense that bringing people together to find nonviolent solutions to their conflicts is difficult. There are powerful reasons why we might want to continue our conflicts, even if resolving them would bring positive benefits to us and our people.

So what can we do? Are there any ways to use these insights to help make the resolution of conflicts more likely? If people insist on engaging in conflicts, it may well be difficult to stop them. But if identity concerns drive some of the persistence of nationalist conflicts, interventions aimed at addressing those identity concerns might take some of the vehemence out of the conflicts. There are a number of specific avenues we might take in negotiations if we want to maximize the chances that the negotiations will succeed. The next chapter describes such an approach to negotiation.

Chapter 6

IMPLICATIONS FOR NEGOTIATIONS

I have argued so far that all of the primary features of nationalist conflict—a strong identification with a national group, assertions that the group has rights to a particular place, a perception of threat from others, and a reluctance to give up the nationalist struggle—can be intensified, if not created outright, by concerns about identity. In fact, identity concerns can be so important to us that at times it might seem more important to us to fight than to make peace, even if we and our loved ones are suffering from that fight. And indeed, nationalist conflicts are notoriously tenacious. In Sri Lanka there have been three significant rounds of peace talks—in 1987, 1989-1990, and 1994-1995—and at this writing (in May 2001) there are discussions about beginning new ones. However, each of these talks to date has collapsed amid accusations that one side or the other was not really serious about wanting to end the conflict.[1] The Armenia/Azerbaijan conflict continues to be at a stalemate, with ethnic Armenian troops occupying a large part of Azerbaijan, and there is no immediate prospect of coming to a resolution about either the economic isolation of Armenia or the fate of the thousands of refugees in camps across Azerbaijan.

Given the attachment we have to victimhood and the sense that only justice on *our* terms will be acceptable, and given the very real and very difficult strategic, military, and geopolitical contexts of nationalist conflict, it is not surprising that attempts to find a final resolution to the Sri Lankan and Armenia/Azerbaijan conflicts have been elusive. However, there are times when, either through their own recognition of the price of the conflict, or through pressure brought on them by others, participants in conflicts such as these come together to negotiate. If that happens, what kinds of actions might help facilitate the success of these negotiations, and what kinds will impede it? I argued in the last chapter that because of the nature of identity, we as human beings are always constantly on the lookout for any sign of disrespect or threat. We are also always seeking ways to be right.

Given these basic ideas, two principles follow: First, any action that conveys a lack of respect for the other party or threatens their identity will undermine negotiations, and any action that conveys respect for the other party or supports their identity will make negotiations more productive. Second, since all parties in negotiations will want to obtain the just solution they believe they deserve, finding a way to meet the needs for perceived justice may provide an opening to resolving the conflict. This chapter gives some examples of how these principles might operate in real negotiations.

Respect and Disrespect

An example from my Psychology of Nationalism course might help to illustrate how groups' perceptions of disrespect can interfere with a negotiating process. In one of the group work sessions, I pitted two groups against each other in a win–lose situation. One, the Smooth Operators, had to obtain an envelope that was located down the hall from the classroom. Another, Three Girls and a Guy, (3GG) had been told that their task was to prevent the Smooth Operators from completing their task, whatever it may be. At one point during the class session, Brenda,[2] a member of the Smooth Operators, went out into the hall to get the envelope. She was followed by Alice, a member of 3GG. When Brenda found the envelope, Alice rushed at her and grabbed the envelope out of her hand. Brenda, in return, then chased Alice into the Psychology Department office and attempted to grab the envelope back. Unfortunately (for her) she was prevented from doing so by the department secretary (who, understandably, did not want students fighting in her office). The result was that 3GG completed their task, and the Smooth Operators did not.

The Smooth Operators were upset that they had lost their reward, and in the next group session wrote a grievance against 3GG for using force against them. When asked why they thought 3GG did this action, they wrote that in addition to stopping the Smooth Operators from completing their task, 3GG did it "to be obnoxious and make other groups angry." When asked how 3GG would probably react to this grievance, the Smooth

Operators wrote: "They won't really care, or they'll be proud of them-selves." Although 3GG had been victorious, they also were upset, believing that the Smooth Operators had harassed their group member in the department office. The members of the two groups were quite angry at each other.

In order to try to redress the anger the two groups felt toward each other, I set up a mediation session. Representatives of the two groups came together in the center of the room, with a neutral mediator approved by both groups (a member of the "Styxx," a third student group). It quickly became clear that each side wanted apologies from the other. The Smooth Operators wanted 3GG to apologize for using force against them and stealing the letter, while 3GG wanted the Smooth Oper-ators to apologize for Brenda's "attacking" Alice in order to get the letter back. After an hour of negotiation, the two sides produced the following agreement:

> We, the undersigned, agree that we were both wrong to commit violent acts. The tactics used were not appropriate.

> Three Girls and a Guy will receive a formal written apology from the Smooth Operators.

> Smooth Operators will receive a formal written apology from Three Girls and a Guy, including a separate apology from Alice in which she admits she was wrong.

> This treaty is signed in the hope of preventing violence in the future.

The treaty was signed by the representatives of both groups and the mediator.

When the two sides attempted to put the treaty into action, however, there was a problem. Both sides wrote their apologies, but the Smooth Operators did not like the tone of the two apologies provided by 3GG. The group's apology was the following:

> We, Three Girls and a Guy, apologize to the "Smooth" Operators for actions taken against them on 13 April 1999. Although the tactics used were not apropos, they were deemed necessary to complete our task, even if we were later screwed by the one who makes the rules.[3] We were wrong.

This apology was accompanied by one from Alice, which read:

Smooth Operators—

So sorry—formally, for taking the Smooth Operators' task. I was wrong in the way that I went about procuring it.

Alice

The Smooth Operators objected to the tone of these apologies, saying that they did not sound sincere (note the quotation marks around "Smooth" and the justification of 3GG's actions in the first apology). This objection caused the talks to break down again. The class period then ended, and the groups came back during the next class period and began the negotiations again. After another hour of discussions, 3GG rewrote their apologies as follows:

We, Three Girls and a Guy, formally apologize to the Smooth Operators for the actions taken against them on April 13th, 1999. We admit that the fact that Alice took the envelope from Brenda was inappropriate. Our task was to prevent the Smooth Operators from completing their task. However, the means by which we attempted to complete our task was not well thought out. We also apologize that our previous apology did not adequately convey the sincerity of our intentions. In writing this, we hope to restore communication between ourselves and the Smooth Operators.

I, Alice Johnson, sincerely apologize for the force I used in taking the sheet from Brenda's hand. It was wrong, and for this I apologize and hope that my relations with the Smooth Operators will not be affected because of it.

The Smooth Operators accepted these apologies, and the conflict between the two groups was more or less resolved. Some of the irritation and anger remained, however, even at the end of the semester when all of this was past history.

The Point

Obviously, the stakes in these negotiations were nothing like those in a real-life nationalist conflict. No one was physically in danger (despite the claims of the groups about violence), and no one lost his or her house or land.

The actual harm experienced by the Smooth Operators was minimal. Yet even though the issues involved were trivial, the people involved had an extremely hard time letting go of the injury they had felt.

What this example illustrates is how easily the self-images and self-esteem of groups can become an issue in negotiations that are ostensibly directed toward an entirely different issue. Here the negotiations were intended to address the grievance that the Smooth Operators had against 3GG for stealing the envelope. However, that substantive issue quickly got lost, and the negotiations became derailed into examinations of the sincerity of the apologies written. In fact, the Smooth Operators/3GG negotiations bear striking similarity to the negotiations that the U.S. government held with the Chinese government in the wake of a collision between an American spy plane and a Chinese fighter jet in April, 2001. After the collision, the spy plane entered Chinese airspace and landed safely, while the fighter jet and pilot were lost.

The ostensible issue of these negotiations was initially the fate of the American crew in Chinese custody, and the attribution of responsibility for the incident. But the release of the crew was delayed for several days when the Chinese government began by demanding an apology from the United States, which the U.S. government refused to give. Then American officials began to offer expressions of "regret."[4] However, the Chinese found that expression unacceptable, particularly because it was translated into a Chinese word that did not include a sense of guilt[5]. Further negotiations ensued, and the United States eventually issued a note in which the U.S. Ambassador to China expressed "sincere regret" over the loss of the pilot and said that the U.S. government was "very sorry" for the loss that the Chinese people and the pilot's family had experienced.[6] The American crew was then freed.

Why, in both these situations, was so much energy expended on negotiating the exact wording of these apologies? First of all, remember that incidents such as these are only partly physical. An apology is an attempt to rectify not only the physical loss that an aggrieved group has suffered, but also the *psychological* injury of not being respected by the aggressor (in the Chinese case, this included not only the loss of a pilot, but the encroachment onto China's airspace and territory). In psychological terms, receiving an apology is a very important act. It demonstrates that the aggressor now feels respect for the aggrieved. It also confirms the victim status of the aggrieved group and allows its members to retain their sense of moral justification. However, if the apology is not sincere, then the relationship cannot be repaired. The perceived lack of sincerity in 3GG's first apology demonstrated to the Smooth Operators that 3GG did not respect them sufficiently. The expressions of "regret" from the United States to China may well have been interpreted the same way.

The suggestion that relationship issues underlie "substantive" issues such as territory or resources, and that those underlying issues must be addressed in negotiation, is an idea discussed by a number of those who have studied conflict resolution.[7] Max Kampelman, the lead U.S. negotiator for the arms-reduction talks with the Soviet Union in the 1980s, has described how he interacted in the negotiation sessions with his Soviet counterparts.[8] It is crucial, he says, to respect the person you are negotiating with. We do not necessarily need to *agree* with everything that our opponent asserts (and indeed, Kampelman disagreed with much that the Soviet delegation had to say), but there is nothing to be gained from embarrassing one's adversaries or making them lose face. And indeed, this suggestion has been borne out in recent research.[9] The idea here is consistent: If both parties do not feel that their honor or dignity is being attacked, they are more likely to engage in discussions about the substantive issues at the table.

Legitimacy

There are a number of ways that issues of respect might arise in negotiations. First and foremost is the according of full recognition to each party in the negotiations as a legitimate partner or participant. Because in many situations one party (such as a secessionist group) may be seen as illegitimate by the other party (such as the government), this can be a very difficult issue. At the same time, establishing the legitimacy of the negotiating parties cannot be avoided. If identity issues are involved in a nationalist struggle, which I have argued they are, then we would expect that the nationalist group will in some ways be attuned to any sign of what it perceives to be disrespect or lack of consideration from the other group. If such identity concerns are not addressed, then they can perhaps even derail negotiations entirely.

For example, from September 1994 to December 1995 the government of Sri Lanka, headed by Chandrika Bandaranaike Kumaratunga, engaged in negotiations with the LTTE, headed by Velupillai Pirabakaran,[10] with the aim of ending the conflict. There were four actual meetings between representatives of the two sides, plus a number of letters exchanged via the International Committee of the Red Cross. One issue that arose early in the talks was the composition of the negotiating teams. The first negotiating team sent by the Sri Lankan government included four men, none of whom were senior government officials. The LTTE's chief ideologue, Anton Balasingham, described the LTTE leader's reaction to the government negotiating team this way:

> Having scrutinized the list of nominees, Mr. Pirabakaran told me that Chandrika was neither serious nor earnest in seeking a peace dialogue with the Tamil Tigers. The LTTE leader felt that the Kumaratunga government was treating the Tamil Tigers as an illegal rebel movement functioning outside the framework of constitutional politics, not as a liberation organization representing the Tamil nation. There would be no parity between the parties in conflict at the negotiating table. By nominating a low-key team without political knowledge or power, we felt the government was deliberately devaluing the significance of the direct negotiations.[11]

Here, the LTTE understood the composition of the negotiating team to be a challenge to the LTTE's legitimacy as a negotiating party, and, indeed, as a representative of the Tamil people. The LTTE, however, believes itself to be more than just a militant group and more than just a political party. They see themselves as the spokespeople for the Tamil nation and as the future government of an independent Tamil Eelam.[12] It appears that the potential success of these negotiations was already compromised because identity issues were not addressed directly at the outset. Those negotiations eventually failed. In analyzing the failure of the negotiations, Balasingham notes again the composition of the government's negotiating team and says that this was aimed at "belittling" direct negotiations in favor of the exchange of letters. He then describes those letters by saying:

> The letters contributed to the gradual build up of distrust and hostility and also helped to reinforce the mutually entrenched positions widening the gap between the protagonists. Written in an over-patronizing and condescending tone, some of the government's letters displayed the arrogance of the state authority treating the opponent (the LTTE) as inferior. Implicit in these letters was a denial to the Tamil Tigers the equal status of a combatant in armed conflict in a national liberation war. This aspect was a major irritant, compelling the LTTE leadership to respond with bitterness and hostility.[13]

Thus progress on important issues in the talks, such as the economic embargo on the north and military movements by both sides, was significantly hindered by this underlying and unresolved issue of respect and legitimacy.

Legitimacy can also be brought up in more subtle ways, by the choice of words that the participants in a conflict use to describe each other. Sinhalese nationalists often make the point that the conflict in Sri Lanka is a "terrorist" conflict and not a nationalist or ethnic one at all. If it were an ethnic conflict, they argue, then why can so many Tamils live peacefully in Colombo and other areas of Sri Lanka? Those who are fighting, they say, are terrorists who are doing so either for their own private gain or because they have been pressured or intimidated into fighting by the LTTE. The solution to the conflict is clear: Eliminate the terrorists militarily, and the peoples of Sri Lanka could finally live in peace.[14] This kind of language takes anyone who might advocate a separate state for Tamils and labels them "terrorists" who should be attacked, not negotiated with. The LTTE also does its part to undermine the Sri Lankan government's legitimacy. Close to the end of the negotiations in 1995, the LTTE sent a memorandum to President Kumaratunga that began, "Yours is a Government that came from the mandate of the Sinhala people to resolve the ethnic conflict."[15] The implication of this statement is that Kumaratunga is not the representative of the *peoples* of Sri Lanka, only of one part of them, an image that would undercut the identity of any leader of a multicultural state. In his "Heroes' Day Message" of November 2000, the leader of the LTTE suggests that the Kumaratunga government assumed power fraudulently, and he uses terms such as "chauvinists" and "racists" and "quisling group" to describe supporters of the ruling party.[16] These words carry a heavy negative content and may well influence the thinking of those who hear them. Indeed, that is the whole point of propaganda pieces like these.

It is easy to see why conflicting groups might use this kind of language in their public statements and propaganda; it does a good job of discrediting their opponents. However, such rhetoric creates potential difficulties for negotiations. If a government enters into negotiations with a group it describes as a simple terrorist organization with no real mandate to represent anyone, then, in the absence of some kind of external pressure, why would that group want to negotiate seriously? Similarly, if a separatist group denies the legitimacy of a government, why would the government want to take the risk of negotiations? In order to have negotiations work, those involved must not feel that their identities are threatened; otherwise, they will spend their time defending their identities rather than negotiating over the issues at hand.

Legitimacy and Self-Determination

The problem, of course, is that acknowledging the legitimacy of the other is often very closely linked, in nationalist conflicts, with the issue of self-determination—the right for a group to decide how to govern itself. For example, many of the mediation attempts to resolve the Nagorno-Karabakh conflict have been conducted by the Minsk group of the Organization for Security and Cooperation in Europe (OSCE).[17] In 1995, the OSCE convened negotiations in Moscow that were designed to bring resolution to the Nagorno-Karabakh conflict. One of the most contentious issues in setting up those negotiations was whether or not Nagorno-Karabakh itself would be a party to those talks. Azerbaijan insisted that since Nagorno-Karabakh was not an independent entity, it should not have a place in negotiations, and that the primary negotiations should be between Azerbaijan and Armenia. Armenia believed otherwise. In this case, the issue is identity integrity at its most obvious: Are the Nagorno-Karabakh Armenians a coherent and distinct entity, worthy of an equal place at the negotiating table, or are they simply Armenians, indistinguishable from the Armenians in Armenia?

This is a complex issue, because whether or not Nagorno-Karabakh Armenians should be considered an independent entity is the ultimate issue to be decided in the talks. Omitting Nagorno-Karabakh from the talks would be difficult, since Nagorno-Karabakh and its people are central to the conflict. On the other hand, it is understandable why Azerbaijan would be reluctant to have Nagorno-Karabakh as an equal party in the talks, since Azerbaijan does not believe that Nagorno-Karabakh has legitimacy as an entity separate from the Azerbaijani state. As of this writing, representatives of Nagorno-Karabakh have been present at the Minsk group negotiations but have not been accorded the status of a full participant. Indeed, there have been some peace proposals that have been agreed to in principle by the governments of Armenia and Azerbaijan but have been rejected by Nagorno-Karabakh.[18]

These difficulties arise because of the association of self-determination with secession. Though the phrase "respect for the principle of equal rights and self-determination of peoples" appears twice in the United Nations Charter, there has been considerable discussion about whether or not that phrase should be interpreted as meaning that any people should have the right to secede from an established state. The position of the United States has always been that self-determination does not mean the right to secession, and many others have agreed.[19] However, as I noted in chapter 3, the nation-state has been privileged in many ways in the modern international system. Given the prominence of the nation-state as a way of protecting a national group and achieving recognition for its identity, it is not strange that those involved in nationalist movements might equate a fully recognized identity with the achievement of a nation-state.

And yet there is no inherent reason why the full recognition of a people as a unique and cohesive group should mean that they must necessarily have their own state. It is possible, for example, for the Sri Lankan government to say to the Tamil people that it recognizes that the Sri Lankan Tamils have a unique society and culture that deserves to be protected and promoted, and that they have a right to substantial say over their destiny as a people, while at the same time declining to support the establishment of a Sri Lankan Tamil state. Similarly, the LTTE (or other Tamil organizations) can acknowledge the historical connection between Theravada Buddhism and the island of Sri Lanka without accepting the conclusion that Sri Lanka must therefore be a Buddhist state. Of course, this is easy to say from the vantage point of a people who have *already* achieved a nation-state than of those who are struggling to achieve one. But the main point is that establishing respect for the identity of the other is primary, and discussions about the form that such legitimacy should take are grounded on that legitimacy being accepted first.

Indeed, this is exactly the approach that has been advocated by some in interventions into the Israeli-Palestinian conflict.[20] Since that conflict consists of two peoples who each say that they have the right to live in a particular territory, there has been a tendency to assume that only one of the two peoples could be acknowledged as having true nationhood. If one is acknowledged as being a legitimate nation with a historical tie to the land, then the other must be excluded. Viewing national identity as an either-or proposition, in which the Israelis' right to exist was seen as being antithetical to the Palestinians' right to exist (and vice-versa), was a large obstacle to resolving that conflict, until 1993 when the two peoples formally acknowledged each other's right to exist.[21] But in fact, the reality is that *both* peoples have a historical tie to the land, and both have claims to nationhood. It is far more realistic to acknowledge the integrity of both national identities, and to suggest that how that nationhood is *expressed*—via a sovereign state, or autonomy within another state, or by some other means—must develop through negotiations between the peoples involved.[22]

These principles are equally applicable to the Armenia-Azerbaijan conflict and the Sri Lankan conflict. In each of these there are peoples (or individuals representing them) asserting the right to be recognized as coherent and unique nations. Azerbaijanis, Armenians, Nagorno-Karabakh Armenians, Sinhalese, and Sri Lankan Tamils all have claims to nationhood. And they all have the right to be treated with respect and with the recognition of their uniqueness and worth. That does not necessarily mean that each of those groups should have a state devoted to protecting their identity. But it does mean that if those involved want negotiations to be successful, then supporting the integrity of those national identities is one way to help such success happen.

Above I noted that those actions likely to be perceived as threatening to identity would disrupt negotiations, whereas any actions that support identity should facilitate them. Explicitly acknowledging the legitimacy of the groups involved and of their representatives is one concrete way of showing which such support. However, there are other more subtle ways in which identity issues can arise in negotiations or discussions. Particularly sensitive points for identity include territory and language.

Territory

Territory is a prime issue in many nationalist conflicts, particularly in secessionist conflicts in which an ethnic group claims a particular territory as its own. Territory clearly can have strategic dimensions. In Nagorno-Karabakh there is an ancient fortress city known as Shusha that sits on a high hill overlooking the capital of Nagorno-Karabakh, Stepanakert. During the war over Nagorno-Karabakh it was occupied by Azerbaijanis (as it was before the war), who used it to shoot missiles into Stepanakert. Whoever controls Shusha thus has a strategic advantage. Similarly, control over territory can mean control over resources, such as oil or agricultural land, or it might mean the ability to blockade another territory and prevent access to it.

Yet territory can have significant psychological dimensions too. An attachment to a particular territory is, after all, one central aspect of national identity. If we as human beings tend to be sensitive to potential threats to identity, then discussions of territory are likely to provide a particularly sensitive flashpoint when the combatant parties are talking to one another. An example that might showcase this is the Sri Lankan government's policy of settling Sinhalese people in the Dry Zone in the north of Sri Lanka. The Dry Zone is arid land that is understood by many Tamils to be a part of their historical territory.[23] However, beginning in the 1930s,[24] there has been a large increase in the Sinhalese population there, due to Sinhalese people being settled with government help and support, such as free land and free irrigation.[25] This change in population has brought with it a variety of practical and political implications for the people who were already living there, such as determining who gets access to needed materials and who represents districts with changing ethnic proportions. However, there are also psychological implications to this change. Tamil nationalists call this settlement "colonization" [26] of their traditional lands, and it is more than just a practical issue—it is a psychological invasion, a threat to the integrity of their identity as a people. The Dry Zone was a key issue in Tamil political platforms in 1956, 1960, and 1976,[27] and it continues to be so today. In his 2000 Heroes' Day speech, the leader of the LTTE said:

> The Tamils of Eelam have a unique ethnic identity. They are a community of people constituted as a national formation experiencing a national consciousness of their own. They have their own lands; a historically constituted territory which is their homeland. Our people desire only one thing. They want to live happily in peace in their own lands without being dominated or harassed by others. The deepest aspiration of our people is to live in dignity in a political environment where they could rule themselves. The Sinhalese should try to understand the Tamil aspirations. It is on the basis of this understanding [that] a just and permanent solution could be built up.[28]

In this statement Pirabakaran identifies Tamil aspirations very closely with their traditional territory. The Tamils are not the only ones attached to their territory, of course. Sinhalese nationalists fear the establishment of Tamil Eelam as an encroachment on their own land, particularly since the proposed state would occupy much of the rich coastline of Sri Lanka. The point is that territory and identity are closely intertwined.

Another example comes from the Armenia-Azerbaijan conflict. One unlikely suggestion for ending the conflict in Nagorno-Karabakh would be to trade Nagorno-Karabakh for Nakhchivan.[29] As can be seen from the map, Nakhchivan is a part of Azerbaijan that is separated from the rest of Azerbaijan by a strip of Armenia. It provides a direct link between Azerbaijan and Turkey. However, since the war, it has been unreachable from

Azerbaijan except by air, because Armenia controls the rail line that runs along the Armenia-Iran border. The two areas, Nakhchivan and Nagorno-Karabakh, are relatively equal in size. Couldn't Nagorno-Karabakh be assigned back to Azerbaijan, and Nakhchivan be given to Armenia? Wouldn't that solve a good number of the problems in the conflict?

Unfortunately, this suggestion would not work. Though territory is certainly a resource, it cannot simply be traded as if it were some kind of commodity. Beyond the concern that the international community would not approve of the wholesale changing of established borders, Armenians and Azerbaijanis alike would protest. These territories have strong emotional attachments for the people involved. We have seen the attachment of the Karabakh Armenians to that land. Nakhchivan is the home of a number of Azerbaijani leaders, and the Azerbaijanis see it as a historically important Azerbaijani land (as do Armenians).[30] In negotiations over buying a house or a car, for example, we might well start with a high demand, expecting that eventually we would lessen it and come to a compromise. But negotiations dealing with historical territory cannot proceed like that. An opening demand, even if it were a negotiating ploy, might well be seen as a threat, which would in turn undermine the possibility for future progress in negotiations.

So territory needs to be seen in its psychological as well as strategic and practical terms, and those psychological aspects need to be acknowledged. Another psychological issue that arises in negotiations is how to deal with historical grievances.

Historical Grievances

Most groups that have been engaged in violent conflict will have had traumatic experiences with each other. In the last chapter, I argued that these historical traumas can provide a sense of victimization to a people, which, in turn, can provide them with a sense of moral justification. For that reason, as a part of negotiations, aggrieved peoples may well be expected to insist that their victimization be recognized. Their opponents in negotiation may not want to give such recognition for fear that it will be used to justify the demands that the other side is making. How can such sticking points be addressed?

Psychological work in conflict resolution has suggested that airing such historical grievances is an important part of bringing warring parties together. One approach to conflict resolution used by psychologists has been "problem-solving workshops."[31] In these workshops, unofficial representatives of conflicting sides meet in a neutral location for three to five days in order to come up with ideas for resolving the conflicts in which they are embroiled. These workshops have been conducted with Israelis and Egyptians, Israelis and Palestinians, and representatives of Protestants and Catholics in Northern Ireland, among others. In such workshops, one phenomenon that often occurs is that participants want, early on, to express their groups' historical grievances against each other.[32] Given the importance of recognizing historical traumas, this is not surprising. However, it is also not surprising that each side in the negotiations may have trouble listening to the other side's grievances (and the accusations they might well contain) or accepting them. Nonetheless, it is important for such grievances to be aired and to be heard, because a resistance to listening to such grievances may be interpreted as a denial of their importance or their legitimacy. Because those historical traumas may be a significant aspect of the aggrieved group's identity, the refusal to hear or accept the traumas is, in a sense, a denial of the legitimacy of the group itself. Indeed, the need to have one's traumas acknowledged was a major reason for setting up the Truth and Reconciliation Commission in South Africa after the move away from apartheid.[33]

There are many examples of historical traumas that might arise in negotiations aimed at ending conflicts, such as the 1915 massacres in Turkey for the Armenians, the events at Khojaly in 1992 for the Azerbaijanis, and others. But less vivid events can also serve as historical traumas. In Sri Lanka in 1956, the government passed the Sinhala Only Act, which made Sinhalese the official language of Sri Lanka instead of English. This act effectively stripped the livelihood from the many Tamils who worked in the civil service, using English as a common language with their Sinhalese counterparts. On the one hand, this policy amounted to clear economic discrimination, since Tamils who could not speak Sinhalese found themselves out of a job. However, it also left a lasting impression that seems to go beyond its immediate economic impact. The Sinhala Only Act is still cited widely as one of the major attacks on the integrity of Sri Lankan Tamils in recent history,[34] and language has been a central part of many of the major negotiations between Sinhalese and Tamil political parties over the past 50 years.[35]

Thus the economic discrimination inherent in the Sinhala Only Act and subsequent language discrimination may be overshadowed by their potential to make Tamils in Sri Lanka feel disrespected and unacknowledged. Even though this act is no longer in force, it still plays a role in the consciousness of Tamil groups in Sri Lanka. How can the damage of such a historical grievance be addressed now, 50 years later?

In recent years it has become common for public apologies to be made, and, in some cases, reparations to be paid for such historical traumas. Reparations have been paid to Japanese-Americans interned during World War II, Jewish survivors of the Holocaust, and others.[36] Public apologies can go a long way to providing the sense of justice that aggrieved peoples so commonly have. At the same time, as in the case of 3GG and the Smooth Operators, it may well be that such apologies will not be accepted if the aggrieved party does not feel that they are sincere. And untangling the legal issues can be difficult also. In 1995, for example, the foreign ministers of Germany and the Czech Republic signed a declaration that provided apologies from each side for the German annexation of the Sudetenland during World War II and for the Czech killings of thousands of Germans afterward. The apologies took time to craft, since both sides wanted to acknowledge their responsibility but not open themselves up to legal claims for reparations.[37] But to the extent that an apology provides a sense of justice, it may help to reinforce the identity needs of the aggrieved party or parties. And in doing so, an apology may help remove historical traumas as a sticking point in negotiations.

Overall, how can the demand for acknowledgement of historical grievances be understood? First of all, in most cases these historical traumas were times during which the physical survival of a substantial number of group members was either threatened or attacked, and so these events were both physical and psychological threats at the same time. When the aggrieved group calls for acknowledgement, in some sense they are calling for an affirmation of their experience as a people, an affirmation of aspects of their identity that they see as central. If the historical atrocity is not acknowledged by the perpetrator, or indeed by the larger world community, that is tantamount to a deep denial of the group's legitimacy and identity.

Thus I would argue that when a group brings up a historical trauma in a negotiating context, what the members of that group really want is acknowledgement—an acknowledgement that their historical experience as a people, and as individuals, is accepted as genuine. Such an acknowledgement would serve to confirm the cohesiveness of their identity as a people, just as the lack of acknowledgement is, in some sense, a denial of that identity.

Addressing Identity Concerns

In discussing all of these issues I have argued that identity dimensions are intertwined with the issues to be negotiated. We demand acknowledgements of our historical traumas because without them we feel that we are being disrespected or ignored. We demand territory because possession of territory acknowledges us as a cohesive people. We demand to be treated as equals because such treatment gives us the dignity and respect that any people deserve. But these are very complex issues. In Sri Lanka, part of very problem that the Sri Lankan government is dealing with is whether or not to treat the LTTE as the sole representative of the Tamil people, as the LTTE insists. Exactly who the "historical" inhabitants of Nagorno-Karabakh are is similarly central to the Nagorno-Karabakh conflict. How can these issues be addressed at the psychological level without prescribing particular solutions to the territorial, language, and responsibility issues that are legitimately part of the negotiation process?

I would argue that there are three major arenas in which the acknowl-edgement and support of identity can take place: in the negotiation process itself, in the public discourse within the conflicting societies, and in the way we speak about nationalist struggles in the broader international context. The first arena, the negotiation process, has been discussed above. The prin-ciples I have put forward—respecting the integrity of one's counterparts, avoiding language that undermines or threatens their identity, and attempt-ing to understand their concerns fully—are not new; they can be seen in many writings on conflict resolution and mediation.[38] Respecting a peo-ple's identity is similar to the concept of allowing individuals to "save face" in negotiations.[39] Paying attention to the language we use, being aware of how our phrasing can exacerbate or ease conflict, plays a significant role in conflict resolution in couples.[40] And separating personal issues (such as identity) from the other substantive issues in negotiations is a central theme in much of current negotiation literature.[41]

In societies in which nationalist conflicts are occurring, however, there is more to conflict resolution than actual negotiation processes. After all, nationalism extends beyond the leaders and elites who might be involved in negotiations. The populace might participate by voting (or not voting), by engaging in riots or pogroms, or by supporting separatist groups finan-cially. So if there is to be resolution of a nationalist conflict within a soci-ety, we have to look beyond the behavior of the negotiators. We need to look also at the rhetoric used by the media and by leaders within the soci-ety or societies involved to see what kind of public discourse might pave the way for conflict resolution to be possible.

The social discourse in society occurs in many ways. Governments shape the way that people understand themselves and their history through propaganda campaigns, attempts to control the media, and even through constructing or influencing the curricula that children study in school. Nationalist groups conduct their own propaganda campaigns. And as I noted above, the same techniques that make for strong propaganda can do much to reduce the possibility of resolving a conflict. Statements that threaten or undermine identity, that deny legitimacy to either side, or that demonstrate disrespect for a people will exacerbate conflict.

In fact, any rhetoric that facilitates ingroup-outgroup phenomena will also exacerbate conflict. Remember from chapter 1 that human beings easily engage in such phenomena—denigrating outgroups, demonizing other people, believing only the worst about them. In fact, we do so at the slightest provocation. And once we have a devalued image of the "enemy," then we tend to remember information that is consistent with that image and not to remember information that clashes with it. We therefore need to be careful about the images we create of each other, because once they are created they tend to have a life of their own. A negative image of a national minority, for example, may lead people to believe that if some kind of atrocity happens, it must be the fault of that group. It may seem obvious to say this, but rhetoric that is inclusive, that supports the identity of national minorities and suggests that they have a place in society, is more likely to facilitate communication than is rhetoric that is combative. The point here is that public discourse about the "other" can have an effect on how the majority and the minority view themselves and how they view each other.

And finally, this analysis has implications for how we talk about identity in the international sphere. I would suggest that given the large role that identity plays in fostering nationalist conflict, if we want to reduce communal and nationalist violence, we (meaning all of us in the international community) need to base our actions and our rhetoric on principles that do *not* rely heavily on notions of identity. Statehood is not and should not be the only way that a national group can gain safety and legitimacy. The notion of self-determination, which is included in many international documents, as described above, need not be linked inextricably to secession and statehood.[42] The principle of self-determination, laudable as it may sound and as consistent with our principles as it may be, is a recipe for the escalation and aggravation of small-scale military disputes into full-fledged wars. Finding ways to safeguard the security of national minorities without recourse to statehood would provide broader opportunities for aggrieved groups to achieve their goals.

Conclusion

Some of these ideas may seem either obvious, farfetched, or both. Certainly a reduction in combative rhetoric might help to reduce violent conflict. But how often do governments really engage in such a lessening of rhetoric, when there is so much (in the short term) to be gained from it? We often do not really *want* to reduce conflict, because we are getting something out of it, personally, politically, or both. And that is not surprising. I have spent much of this book arguing that conflict plays some significant psychological roles for us. Therefore we would expect that, except in the most difficult situations, conflict would be very hard to give up—unless we found some other way of meeting our need to feel right and justified and to have our identity feel cohesive, or unless we were pressured into a resolution by someone more powerful. At the societal level, there is little that anyone can do to make people give up conflict, aside from using peacekeeping forces or some other kind of coercion to keep them apart. At an individual level, though, there is much that we can do to make ourselves less prone to nationalist conflict. What we can do as individuals is the subject of the final chapter.

Chapter 7

IS THERE HOPE?

When I talked with refugees in Azerbaijan, I often ended the interview by asking how they would feel if they were able to return to their homes in Nagorno-Karabakh. Would they be able to live side-by-side with their former Armenian neighbors after all that has happened? Most of those I talked to answered that they would like to say that they could live peacefully with Armenians, but in reality their anger and bitterness were so great that a peaceful coexistence might be impossible.

When I later traveled to Nagorno-Karabakh, I asked the same question. Armenians there told me how they barely managed to survive in Stepanakert during the war: the daily bombings they endured from the Azerbaijani forces, the many deaths they witnessed, and the countless other sacrifices that they made to achieve control over that land. They told me very clearly that they would not consent to relinquishing any of the territory they fought so hard to get, no matter what the authorities in Yerevan and Baku might decide.

I left Nagorno-Karabakh very discouraged. It seemed that the only way to achieve a peaceful reintegration of the two groups would be for someone to go from one house to the next through every Karabakh village, conducting what would amount to one-on-one conflict resolution training with every resident, so that they would be able to work through their anger and move past the tragedies that they had endured. Obviously, this would be impractical, if not impossible, and I found myself wondering whether there was any possibility for peace at all. The political leaders in Armenia and Azerbaijan might eventually come to an agreement that would provide some kind of semi-autonomous status for Nagorno-Karabakh, and perhaps the return of some of the refugees. But the people who would actually have to *live* with such an agreement would be those in the disputed area itself. And their feelings are so strong, their victimization so recent and so vivid, and their sense of the justice of their cause so acute, that I doubted that they would ever be able to achieve a lasting peace.

The situation in Sri Lanka is similarly daunting. Sri Lankan society has undergone tremendous trauma in the last 20 years. I have visited some of the places where innocent bystanders were killed by suicide bombers, where Tamils were killed by mobs, and where radical Sinhalese youth and the government left burning bodies and decapitated heads to send each other messages about their seriousness. Sri Lanka is a small island; no matter what kind of political solution is reached, Tamils and Sinhalese will live in close proximity to one another. And the Tamil and Sinhalese communities are anything but monolithic; there are deep internal divisions within each group that will also have to be faced. The traumas that have befallen Sri Lanka will reverberate for many years. How can people who have undergone such tragedy come together to forge a peace?

One way or another, for these two conflicts to move beyond their current stalemates, those involved will have to live together. The same is true of nearly any nationalist conflict. But I have spent much of this book talking about the human attraction to national identity due to the needs that it meets. When these psychological dynamics are combined with the violence, destruction, and trauma that often accompany nationalist movements, it seems as though the chances for peaceful coexistence are remote. In the face of this powerful combination of psychological needs and historical circumstances, is there hope for change?

Throughout this book I have used psychological research to argue that the tendency to get involved in group conflict is a part of being human. We all categorize, we all identify with social groups, we all engage in ingroup-outgroup behavior, and we do so at least in part because we all struggle with the same need to have a positive and integrated sense of self. Since ingroup-outgroup phenomena are natural human processes, and since the international system privileges national identity as a way to gain self-esteem, nationalist conflicts are probably inevitable. But I do not want to leave this discussion with the implication that we as humans are doomed to be caught in intractable conflicts and that there is no hope for lessening their destructiveness. Even after seeing how deeply we can lock ourselves into conflict, I still believe there is hope. Not all conflicts end with one side simply imposing terms on another; sometimes settlements are negotiated, and people actually do reconcile with one another.

Why do I believe this is the case? If, as I have argued, much of nationalism is about feeling justified, finding a sense of meaning in life, and feeling a part of something larger than ourselves, then moving beyond nationalism would involve finding ways *other* than nationalist conflict to satisfy those needs. I think there are ways we can do so, and this chapter will describe some of them.

The discussion in this chapter is more personal than those in the previous chapters, partly because I have been affected personally by studying nationalism, and partly because the power of the assertions I will make here can best be confirmed not by arguments, but by our own experience. I offer these thoughts as one way of considering how to accept the reality of nationalism and, at the same time, to see the possibilities that lay beyond the conflicts it creates.

Beyond Nationalism

The theoretical argument of this book is that nationalism is one way we fulfill our need to be good, right, just, and a part of something bigger than ourselves. What other ways are there to meet those needs, aside from finding enemies and rallying members of our group to fight them? In chapter 4, I described how the major sources of human insecurity are the aspects of ourselves that we find unacceptable. If that is the case, then the first way to take the power out of nationalism is to accept ourselves as we are. This idea has a long tradition in both psychological and religious thinking. In the context of nationalism, Paul Tillich sums up this point well:

> The most irrevocable expression of the separation of life from life today is the attitude of social groups within nations towards each other, and the attitude of nations themselves towards other nations. The walls of distance, in time and space, have been removed by technical progress; but the walls of estrangement between heart and heart have been incredibly strengthened. The madness of the German Nazis and the cruelty of the lynching mobs in the South provide too easy an excuse for us to turn our thoughts from our own selves. . . . He who is able to love himself is able to love others also; he who has learned to overcome self-contempt has overcome his contempt for others. But the depth of our separation lies in just the fact that we are not capable of a great and merciful divine love towards ourselves.[1]

The world is no less violent now than when Tillich wrote this in 1950, and the psychological dynamics underlying that violence have not changed. Tillich's point is that even though social and political conditions can set the stage for hatred and violence, our feelings about ourselves drive us to *participate* in it. We find it much easier to focus on the evils in others than to accept the evils in ourselves. Correspondingly, our only chance to get out of the cycle of conflict is to accept the reality of who we are, without denying or projecting the parts we do not like.

The central theme of Tillich's statement is compassion—compassion for ourselves as well as for others. In order to be free from the difficult aspects of being human, we need, paradoxically, to accept those aspects with compassion. Doing so can free us from the power that our flaws have had over us. If we are not so driven to prove how good we are, or to demonstrate that we are right and just, or to cleanse ourselves, perhaps some of the psychological power of nationalism will be lessened. This kind of compassion does not mean that we would accept all of our evils and simply perpetuate them on others. On the contrary, just as hatred towards one's self breeds hatred towards others, compassion towards one's self breeds compassion towards others. When our sense of self-worth does not depend on the devaluation and subjugation of others, we are more able to extricate ourselves from the traps of ingroup-outgroup dynamics.

In chapter 5 I identified the need to live a meaningful life as another factor that drives our engagement in nationalism. We can see this in the enthusiastic way that we sometimes engage in war, and in the pride that sacrifice for the good of "the people" can bring. Being a part of a cause is a powerful motivator. Religious teachings have often tried to give people a sense of meaning, purpose, and connection *without* needing a national group to provide it. Christianity teaches that all people are the "children of God." Islam preaches that all people are born Muslim, and it is only through following false teachings that people disobey God. Buddhism and Hinduism teach that the universe is all one whole, and each of us is a part of it, caught on the same wheel of karma.

Unfortunately, the actual *practice* of religious groups has often been to emphasize exclusivity and to foment competition and conflict, just as nationalist groups have done. Just because the idea has been misused, however, does not mean it has no merit. All of these systems of thought converge on the idea that we are, in fact, not so separate and not so isolated from each other as we may believe. In some formulations, the connection between all people is described as mystical, and in others, such as in the environmental movement, it is described in more mundane and prosaic terms. Ultimately, however, the most powerful experience of commonality we share may simply be the undeniable fact that we are all alive, and we will all eventually die. The point is that if we can actually experience a sense of commonality with all other people, then we may be less likely to cling to nationalism as a way to fulfill our need for connection.

Much of this is speculative, of course, and cannot be demonstrated in the same way as some of the other arguments I have made in this book. However, it is undeniable that we as human beings have not yet found easy ways to avoid the destructiveness that comes with group conflict. These suggestions may at least point the way to potentially productive ways of thinking about conflict and its resolution.

Reconciliation

Truly resolving a nationalist conflict means not just ending hostilities, but achieving reconciliation—somehow coming to terms with the injuries we have suffered and inflicted during the conflict, and coming to terms with those who inflicted injuries upon us. As I noted above, it is hard to see how the peoples of Armenia, Azerbaijan, and Sri Lanka will be able to do this, given the many traumas they have suffered through the course of their conflicts. However, there is hope. Individuals in many other conflicts, from small interpersonal conflicts to large nationalist ones, have done so. The social, political, economic, and military factors surrounding the conflicts in Armenia, Azerbaijan, and Sri Lanka will shape how they end, if they do. However, the ultimate resolution of those conflicts will depend on the willingness of the individuals involved to learn to live with their former enemies. The choice of whether and how to do so is theirs. We as observers of nationalist conflicts, and as participants in our own life conflicts, have the opportunity to make our own attempts at peace. As I mentioned in the preface, our task is to develop the compassion and skills necessary to make our interactions with others less destructive. There are many who have done so in the past. Perhaps we can lead the way in the future.

APPENDIX

The Psychology of Nationalism Course

In my Psychology of Nationalism course, I want the students to understand that group identity has implications for everyone, not just people in distant lands who are embroiled in nationalist conflicts. To help the students understand that the same fundamental psychological processes underlie group dynamics everywhere, I divide them into groups, and over the course of the semester they meet in a series of sessions in which they experience intergroup behavior first-hand. After each group work session, the next class period is devoted to discussing the group interactions that arose and the relevant psychological research and thinking about those issues.

The first group work session is devoted to establishing group boundaries. I arrange the chairs in four circles and put masking tape on the floor to indicate the territories of the groups. The group sizes are typically unequal, since unequal group size is a common feature of nationalist conflict. I also give the groups various resources. The group closest to the door has total control over who comes in and out during the group work sessions. Another group controls the telephone. Another group has no resources at all. Again, I do this in order to have the situation mimic reality; in the real world there are nearly always significant power imbalances between groups. I designate a leader for each group, though the groups are able to change leaders in subsequent sessions.

The groups tend to use their resources, or threaten to use them, almost instantly. In the introduction, I described how the Gatekeepers used their size and control over the door to justify their uncompromising and arrogant behavior toward the other groups. In a different semester, Group Yo, a group with no resources at all, creatively used their proximity to the windows to threaten to freeze everyone in the classroom (it was January) unless they got the presentation date they wanted. The group with the telephone is typically able to bargain with the other groups for use of the telephone at some future date, even though no one knows at the beginning of the semester when and even if the telephone will be needed. (That bargaining power was significantly diminished in the most recent semester when a member of Group Yo thought to bring a cell phone to class.)

In the early sessions I introduce activities to help the members of the groups develop a sense of group identity. Each group develops a banner, symbol, and slogan, then explains their meanings to the other groups. The students are often very creative. One year, the group that had control over the door called itself Access Denied, and its banner was a poster that covered the entire doorway with an image of a door covered by a key. In another year, the Smooth Operators used the slogan "It's all within our reach" to illustrate their ability to call anywhere with the class phone.

The groups very quickly begin to develop personalities, characteristic styles of action, and antipathies toward other groups. Students in the class begin to associate the individuals with the stereotypes of their groups. In one semester, a student happened to see a member of Access Denied in a dormitory, fumbling with a key to get into a room, and the student, without thinking, yelled, "You guys can't even open a door!" The students even begin to talk about themselves as though they share the personality characteristics of their group, such as being sneaky, strong, or arrogant.

Several other sessions in the semester are devoted to activities designed to produce intergroup and intragroup conflict. At the beginning of each group work session, I hand out secret memos to each group giving them a task for the day. If a group completes its task, it receives points; if not, it loses them. (The points are vaguely described as redeemable in the future for an unspecified reward.) Some of the assignments, such as to answer obscure questions or locate materials that I have hidden in the psychology building, are designed to provide opportunities for cooperation between the groups if they choose. Others, such as giving one group the task of preventing another group from succeeding at their task, are designed as win-lose situations. The tasks themselves are important only insofar as they provide opportunities for the students to experience what it feels like to be a member of a group and to interact with other groups. Nonetheless, the students tend to take the tasks very seriously throughout the course. They negotiate, collude, bargain, deceive each other, threaten each other, and use a variety of creative means to complete their tasks.

One semester a group called Arcadia had to retrieve a piece of paper with the words "Important Information" from the bulletin board outside my office. The problem was that to do so, they had to get past Athena's Passage, the group with control over the door. In a particularly sneaky (but clever) manipulation, they pretended that one of their members was about to be sick, and Athena's Passage let her out. When she got to my office, she saw that there was a second piece of paper on the bulletin board, obviously intended for another group, and she promptly stole it. The other group, called the Quadlings, then had to negotiate to get it back. The incident left some bad feelings between the groups; Athena's Passage was upset because they had been swindled, and the Quadlings were upset because Arcadia had stolen their task. Arcadia, of course, was very proud of itself. The students' responses to the tasks do not have to do so much with any actual reward they might get. As one student put it in describing her experience in the course, "The points had nothing to do with it. It was all about not looking like a fool!" Individual self-esteem quickly becomes tied to the success of one's group.

Intragroup dynamics are also evident in these sessions. Group members occasionally become dissatisfied with their leader and must decide whether or not to depose him or her. One group called Hot Jambalaya nearly disintegrated because the four members could not consistently support a leader. Dissident factions will also occasionally form. For example, Group Yo (whose slogan was "Angry, Red, and Underappreciated") developed a faction called "La Rouge," which took upon itself the task of attempting covert hostile actions against other groups, such as submitting statements in other groups' names when I asked about the various groups' internal functioning. (To illustrate these issues, I periodically ask the students to diagram both the relationships between the groups and the power hierarchies within their own groups, which helps them understand the roles that individuals can play in shaping intergroup dynamics.)

Naturally, as the groups develop relationships, interact, and compete with each other over the course of the semester, grievances arise. A special session at the end of the semester is devoted to resolving conflicts that arise between the groups. The groups who are in conflict must analyze their situations and choose the form of their negotiations (for example, in whose territory to meet, or inviting a mediator from another group versus having direct talks). As I described in chapter 6, the problems that arise between the groups tend to be, in many ways, trivial. However, the hurt feelings, anger, and resentment are very real, and through the process of attempting to resolve the conflict, the students learn about some of the dynamics that underlie negotiations to end real-life conflicts. The roles of emotions, differing perspectives, and history in perpetuating and resolving nationalist struggles become quite vivid and alive to them.

My hope in offering this course is that the combination of personal experience and academic reflection will help the students to understand nationalism and to have a more compassionate understanding of those who are engaged in nationalist conflict. In the United States it is often easy to believe that nationalist conflict is something that happens to people in other places; through the group work, the students learn that "we" are not so different from "them" after all.

NOTES

Introduction

1. This distinction is drawn from Social Identity Theory (e.g., Tajfel, Henri, *Human Groups and Social Categories: Studies in Social Psychology* (Cambridge, England: Cambridge University Press, 1981).

2. Patricia Carley, *Nagorno-Karabakh: Searching for a Solution* (A United States Institute of Peace Roundtable Report), (Washington, D.C.: United States Institute of Peace, 1998).

3. Michael P. Croissant, *The Armenia-Azerbaijan Conflict: Causes and Implications* (Westport, CT: Praeger, 1998), 139.

4. Arie Vaserman and Rami Ginat, "National, Territorial or Religious Conflict? The Case of Nagorno-Karabakh," *Studies in Conflict and Terrorism* 17 (1994): 345-362.

5. *Sri Lanka: Amnesty International Report 2000.* (London: Amnesty International Publications, 2000).

6. See Stanley J. Tambiah, *Sri Lanka: Ethnic Fratricide and the Dismantling of Democracy* (Chicago: The University of Chicago Press, 1986); and Stanley J. Tambiah, *Leveling Crowds: Ethnonationalist Conflicts and Collective Violence in South Asia* (Berkeley, CA: The University of California Press, 1996), for detailed descriptions.

7. "Lanka Calls for Talks With Tamil Rebels," *The Times of India* 25 January, 2001. Available via the Web at: http://www.timesofindia.com/today/25nbrs2.htm

Chapter One

1. Notable exceptions include Stephen Worchel, *Written in Blood: Ethnic Identity and the Struggle for Human Harmony* (New York: Worth Publishing, 1998); Vamik Volkan, *The Need to Have Enemies and Allies: From Clinical Practice to International Relationships* (Northvale, NJ: Jason Aronson, 1994); Leonard W. Doob, *Patriotism and Nationalism: Their Psychological Foundations* (New Haven: Yale University Press, 1964); and Herbert C. Kelman, "Nationalism, Patriotism, and National Identity: Social-Psychological Dimensions," in *Patriotism: In the Lives of Individuals and Nations,* edited by D. Bar-Tal and E. Staub (Chicago: Nelson-Hall Publishers, 1997).
2. A classic discussion of our tendency to categorize is given in Gordon W. Allport, *The Nature of Prejudice* (Garden City, NY: Doubleday, 1954), from which the general outline of this discussion is taken.
3. For discussions of this point, see Uri Ra'anan, "The Nation-State Fallacy," in *Conflict and Peacemaking in Multiethnic Societies,* edited by J. V. Montville (Lexington, MA: Lexington Books, 1990); and Anthony D. Smith, *National Identity* (London: Penguin Books, 1991), 9-11.
4. Smith, 1991, 11-13.
5. Bryan Pfaffenberger, "Ethnic Conflict and Youth Insurgency in Sri Lanka: The Social Origins of Tamil Separatism," in *Conflict and Peacemaking in Multiethnic Societies,* edited by J. V. Montville (Lexington, MA: Lexington Books, 1991), 247. See also Stanley J. Tambiah, *Sri Lanka: Ethnic Fratricide and the Dismantling of Democracy* (Chicago: The University of Chicago Press, 1986), 5.
6. Tambiah, 1986, 4.
7. Tambiah, 1986, 4.
8. Oddvar Hollup, "The Impact of Land Reforms, Rural Images, and Nationalist Ideology on Plantation Tamils," in *Buddhist Fundamentalism and Minority Identities in Sri Lanka,* edited by T. A. Bartholomeusz and Chandra R. de Silva (Albany, NY: State University of New York Press, 1998).
9. Thomas Goltz, *Azerbaijan Diary : A Rogue Reporter's Adventures in an Oil-Rich, War-Torn, Post-Soviet Republic* (Armonk, NY: M. E. Sharpe, 1999), 175.
10. The Armenian National Assembly, based in Washington, D.C., is an example of an organization that brings together diaspora Armenians.
11. William Graham Sumner, *Folkways; A Study of the Sociological Importance of Usages, Manners, Customs, Mores, and Morals* (Boston: Ginn & Company, 1940) (original work published 1906).
12. See Robert A. LeVine and Donald T. Campbell, *Ethnocentrism: Theories of Conflict, Ethnic Attitudes, and Group Behavior* (New York: John Wiley & Sons, 1972), for an extensive elaboration of this idea.
13. Marilynn B. Brewer, "The Role of Ethnocentrism in Intergroup Conflict," in *Psychology of Intergroup Relations,* ed. S. Worchel and W. C. Austin (Chicago: Nelson-Hall Publishers, 1986).

14. Willem Doise, "An Experimental Investigation into the Formation of Intergroup Representations," *European Journal of Social Psychology* 2 (1972): 202-204.

15. See Marilynn. B. Brewer, "Ingroup Bias in the Minimal Intergroup Situation: A Cognitive-Motivational Analysis," *Psychological Bulletin* 86 (1979), 307-324, for an overview.

16. In this and subsequent chapters I will refer to discussions with Armenians and Azerbaijanis and reproduce quotations from them. I conducted these interviews in Baku, Sabirabad, Yerevan, Chambarak, Stepanakert, and other areas in Armenia and Azerbaijan in late May and early June 2000. The terms of the interviews included anonymity for those who participated, and so none of the quotations will be attributed to specific individuals.

17. Gordon W. Allport, *The Nature of Prejudice* (Garden City, NY: Doubleday, 1954), 21.

18. Charles M. Judd and Bernadette Park, "Out-group Homogeneity: Judgments of Variability at the Individual and Group Levels," *Journal of Personality and Social Psychology* 54 (1988): 778-788.

19. See George Quattrone and Edward E. Jones, "The Perception of Variability within In-groups and Out-groups: Implications for the Law of Small Numbers," *Journal of Personality and Social Psychology* 38 (1980): 141-152.

20. Myron Rothbart, Mark Evans, and Solomon Fulero, "Recall for Confirming Events: Memory Processes and the Maintenance of Social Stereotypes," *Journal of Experimental Social Psychology* 15 (1979), 343-355.

21. Claudia E. Cohen, "Person Categories and Social Perception: Testing Some Boundaries of the Processing Effects of Prior Knowledge," *Journal of Social and Personality Psychology* 40 (1981): 441-452.

22. John W. Howard and Myron Rothbart, "Social Categorization for In-group and Out-group Behavior," *Journal of Social and Personality Psychology* 38 (1980): 301-310.

23. Robyn M. Dawes, David Singer, and Frank Lemons, "An Experimental Analysis of the Contrast Effect and its Implications for Intergroup Communication and the Indirect Assessment of Attitude," *Journal of Personality and Social Psychology* 21 (1972): 281-295.

24. Charles M. Judd and Judith M. Harackiewicz, "Contrast Effects in Attitude Judgment: An Examination of the Accentuation Hypothesis," *Journal of Personality and Social Psychology* 38 (1980): 390-398.

25. Brewer, 1986.

26. Robyn M. Dawes, David Singer, and Frank Lemons, "An Experimental Analysis of the Contrast Effect and its Implications for Intergroup Communication and the Indirect Assessment of Attitude," *Journal of Personality and Social Psychology* 21 (1972), 281.

27. One of the earliest collections of such descriptions was given in Sumner, 1940. His work is reproduced and elaborated upon in LeVine and Camp-

bell, 1972. Summaries of modern work in ingroup-outgroup phenomena are provided by Donelson R. Forsyth, *Group Dynamics,* 3rd ed. (Belmont, CA: Brooks/Cole Publishing Company, 1999); and Marilynn B. Brewer and Norman Miller, *Intergroup Relations* (Pacific Grove, CA: Brooks/Cole Publishing Company, 1996).

28. B. Gaibov and A. Sharifov, *Undeclared War,* trans. Y. Rahimov (Baku: Communist Publishing House, 1991).

29. Sam Keen, *Faces of the Enemy: Reflections of the Hostile Imagination* (New York: Harper & Row, 1988).

30. "Who Wants a Separate State?" A Publication of the Ministry of State, The Government of Sri Lanka; Overseas information Series, No. 9, available via the Web at http://ourworld.compuserve.com/homepages/sinhala/, accessed September 13 2000.

31. Thomas Gilovich, "Seeing the Past in the Present: The Effects of Associations to Familiar Events on Judgments and Decisions," *Journal of Personality and Social Psychology* 40 (1981): 797–808.

32. Anthony R. Pratkanis and Elliot Aronson, *Age of Propaganda: The Everyday Use and Abuse of Persuasion* (New York: W.H. Freeman, 1992), 56.

33. Terry Ann Knopf, *Rumors, Race, and Riots* (New Brunswick: Transaction Books, 1975).

34. Fernand van Langenhove, *The Growth of a Legend: A Study Based upon the German Accounts of Francs-Tireurs and "Atrocities" in Belgium,* trans. E. B. Sherlock (New York: G.P. Putnam's Sons, 1916).

35. Arthur Ponsonby, *Falsehood in War-Time: Containing an Assortment of Lies Circulated Throughout the Nations During the Great War* (New York: E. P. Dutton & Co., Inc., 1928).

36. Van Langenhove, 1916.

37. Ponsonby, 1928.

38. Gordon W. Allport and Leo Postman, *The Psychology of Rumor* (New York: Henry Holt & Company, 1946), 33–34.

39. Allport and Postman, 1946, 34.

40. Ralph L. Rosnow and Gary Alan Fine, *Rumor and Gossip: The Social Psychology of Hearsay* (New York: Elsevier, 1976).

41. Leon Festinger, Dorwin Cartwright, Kathleen Barber, Juliet Fleischl, Josephine Gottsdanker, Annette Keysen, and Gloria Leavitt, "A Study of Rumor: Its Origin and Spread," *Human Relations* 1 (1948): 464–485.

42. Van Langenhove, 1916, has done careful examination of the transmission process of several of the rumors regarding the Belgian *francs-tireurs.*

43. See also Festinger et al., 1948.

44. Tamotsu Shibutani, *Improvised News: A Sociological Study of Rumor* (Indianapolis, IN: The Bobbs-Merrill Company, Inc., 1966).

45. Pratkanis and Aronson, 75. For a review of urban legends that have become widespread after being picked up by news organizations, see John Todd

Llewellyn, "Understanding Urban Legends: A Peculiar Public Relations Challenge," *Public Relations Quarterly* 41 (Winter 1996-1997): 17-22.

46. Goltz, xxiii.

47. Pratkanis and Aronson, 75.

48. Shibutani, 1966.

49. For a description of the massacre, see the Associated Press article, "Sri Lankan Mob Kills 25 Hostage-Takers" (*The Toronto Star*, 26 October 2000: News Section.)

50. For a description, see Waruna Karunatilake, "Two dead as race riots worsen in Hill Country," *The Lanka Academic*, 30 October 2000. Accessible via the Web at http://www.lacnet.org/the_academic/archive/2000_10_30/

51. "Death Toll in Ethnic Violence in Sri Lanka Revised to 362," *New York Times*, 11 August 1983, p. 6. Estimates of the casualties vary widely; the number cited here is from a Sri Lankan government source. At about the same time, the head of a Tamil party claimed that 2,000 people died in the rioting ("Sri Lanka Toll put at 2,000," *New York Times*, 15 August 1983, p. 2.). The exact chain of events, in terms of what caused what, is not clear. See also Stanley J. Tambiah, *Sri Lanka: Ethnic Fratricide and the Dismantling of Democracy* (Chicago: The University of Chicago Press, 1986), 16-17; and Chelvadurai Manogaran, *Ethnic Conflict and Reconciliation in Sri Lanka* (Honolulu: University of Hawaii Press, 1987), 68-69.

52. David Little, *Sri Lanka: The Invention of Enmity* (Washington, D.C.: United States Institute of Peace Press, 1994); see also Tambiah, 1986, 25-27.

53. Samvel Shahmuratian, ed., *The Sumgait Tragedy: Pogroms Against Armenians in Soviet Azerbaijan, Volume I: Eyewitness Accounts* (Cambridge: The Zoryan Institute, 1990). This collection of eyewitness accounts gives detailed stories of a number of the victims of the riots.

54. Stanley J. Tambiah, *Leveling Crowds: Ethnonationalist Conflicts and Collective Violence in South Asia* (Berkeley: The University of California Press, 1996), 96-97.

55. Paul Sieghart, *Sri Lanka—A Mounting Tragedy of Errors* (Report of a mission to Sri Lanka in January 1984 on behalf of the International Commission of Jurists and its British Section, JUSTICE), (London: International Commission of Jurists/JUSTICE, 1984).

56. Shahmuratian, 1990.

57. Igor Nolyain, "Moscow's Initiation of the Azeri-Armenian Conflict," *Central Asian Survey* 13 (1994): 541-563.

Chapter Two

1. "Tamil Inmates Butchered in Sri Lanka Open Prison, Toll 25." News story available at http://www.123India.com: News: Regional, Oct 25 2000, accessed February 2, 2001.

2. Stanley J. Tambiah, *Leveling Crowds: Ethnonationalist Conflicts and Collective Violence in South Asia* (Berkeley: The University of California Press, 1996), 99.

3. Igor Nolyain, "Moscow's Initiation of the Azeri-Armenian Conflict," *Central Asian Survey* 13 (1994): 541-563.

4. Clifford Stott and Steve Reicher, "How Conflict Escalates: The Inter-group Dynamics of Collective Football Crowd Violence," *Sociology* 32 (1998): 353-378.

5. Theodore W. Adorno, Else Frenkel-Brunswick, Daniel J. Levinson, and R. Nevitt Sanford, *The Authoritarian Personality* (New York: Harper & Row, 1950).

6. Abraham H. Maslow, "The Authoritarian Character Structure," *The Journal of Social Psychology, S.P.S.S.I. Bulletin* 18 (1943): 401-411.

7. Gordon W. Allport, *The Nature of Prejudice* (Garden City, NY: Doubleday, 1954), chapter 25.

8. Bob Altemeyer, *The Authoritarian Specter* (Cambridge, MA: Harvard University Press, 1996).

9. Ralph S. Ezekiel, *The Racist Mind: Portraits of American Neo-Nazis and Klansmen* (New York: Viking, 1995).

10. Gordon W. Russell, "Personalities in the Crowd: Those Who Would Escalate a Sports Riot," *Aggressive Behavior* 21 (1995): 91-100.

11. Stanley J. Tambiah, "Friends, Neighbors, Enemies, Strangers: Aggressor and Victim in Civilian Ethnic Riots," *Social Science and Medicine* 45 (1997): 1177-1188.

12. For example, Hugh Donald Forbes, *Nationalism, Ethnocentrism, and Personality* (Chicago: University of Chicago Press, 1985).

13. Ervin Staub, *The Roots of Evil: The Origins of Genocide and Other Group Violence* (Cambridge, UK: Cambridge University Press, 1989), chapter 15.

14. Ervin Staub, "Cultural-Societal Roots of Violence: The Examples of Genocidal Violence and of Contemporary Youth Violence in the United States," *American Psychologist* 51 (1996): 117-132.

15. Firuz Kazemzadeh, *The Struggle for Transcaucasia (1917-1921)* (New York: Philosophical Library, Inc., 1951).

16. Tessa Bartholomeusz, and Chandra R. de Silva, "Buddhist Fundamentalism and Identity in Sri Lanka," in *Buddhist Fundamentalism and Minority Identities in Sri Lanka,* ed. T. J. Bartholomeusz and C. R. de Silva (Albany, NY: State University of New York Press, 1998).

17. John D. Rogers, Jonathan Spencer, and Jayadeva Uyangoda, "Sri Lanka: Political Violence and Ethnic Conflict," *American Psychologist* 53 (1998): 771-777.

18. Chelvadurai Manogaran, *Ethnic Conflict and Reconciliation in Sri Lanka* (Honolulu: University of Hawaii Press, 1987), chapter 2.

19. Muzafer Sherif, *In Common Predicament: Social Psychology of Intergroup Conflict and Cooperation* (Boston: Houghton Mifflin, 1966).

20. Jay W. Jackson, "Realistic Group Conflict Theory: A Review and Evaluation of the Theoretical and Empirical Literature," *The Psychological Record* 43 (1993): 395-414.

21. Sherif, 1966, 82.

22. See, for example, Robert. R. Blake and Jane S. Mouton, "From Theory to Practice in Interface Problem Solving," in S. Worschel and W. G. Austin, eds., *Psychology of Intergroup Relations* (Chicago: Nelson-Hall Publishers, 1986).

23. Manogaran, 1987, 188-121.

24. Zori Balayan, *Between Heaven and Hell: The Struggle for Karabakh,* trans. M. Sapiets, M. Rowe, and F. Corley (Yerevan: Amaras Publishers, 1997; original work published 1995).

25. Rohan Gunaratna, *International and Regional Security Implications of the Sri Lankan Tamil Insurgency* (St. Albans, UK: International Foundation of Sri Lankans, 1997).

26. Gustave LeBon, *Psychologie des Foules (The Crowd).* Trans. and with a new introduction by Robert A. Nye (New Brunswick, NJ: Transaction Publishers, 1995; original work published 1895), 52.

27. Sigmund Freud, *Group Psychology and the Analysis of the Ego,* trans. and ed. J. Strachey (New York: W.W. Norton & Co., 1959; original work published 1922), 9-12, 20.

28. Sheldon J. Lachman, "Psychological Perspective for a Theory of Behavior During Riots," *Psychological Reports* 79 (1996): 739-744.

29. Philip G. Zimbardo, "The Human Choice: Individuation, Reason, and Order Versus Deindividuation," in W. J. Arnold and D. Levine, eds., *Nebraska Symposium on Motivation* 17 (1969): 237-307.

30. See Donelson R. Forsyth, *Group Dynamics* 3rd ed. (Belmont, CA: Brooks/Cole-Wadsworth Publishing Company, 1999, p. 459), for a review of such research.

31. One of the classic studies on this phenomenon is Bibb Latane and John M. Darley, "Group Inhibition of Bystander Intervention in Emergencies," *Journal of Personality and Social Psychology* 10 (1968): 244-268.

32. There is a large amount of psychological research on conformity and other forms of social influence; a summary can be found in Forsyth, 1999, chapter 7.

33. Herbert C. Kelman, "Violence Without Moral Restraint: Reflections on the Dehumanization of Victims and their Victimizers," *Journal of Social Issues* 29 (1973): 25-61.

34. Herbert C. Kelman and V. Lee Hamilton, *Crimes of Obedience: Toward a Social Psychology of Authority and Responsibility* (New Haven: Yale University Press, 1989), 5.

35. Kelman and Hamilton, 1989, 15.

36. For example, see Stanley J. Tambiah, *Sri Lanka: Ethnic Fratricide and the Dismantling of Democracy* (Chicago: The University of Chicago Press, 1986), 24.

37. For one description, see Thomas Goltz, *Azerbaijan Diary: A Rogue Reporter's Adventures in an Oil-Rich, War-Torn, Post-Soviet Republic* (Armonk, NY: M.E.

Sharpe, 1999), chapter 7. A compilation of press reports is provided at "Khojaly," Web site available at http://www.come.to/khojaly/, accessed February 4, 2001.

38. Craig Haney, Curtis Banks, and Philip Zimbardo, "Interpersonal Dynamics in a Simulated Prison," *International Journal of Criminology and Penology* 1 (1973): 69-97.

39. Sigmund Freud, *Civilization and Its Discontents,* trans. J. Strachey (New York: W. W. Norton & Co., 1961; original work published 1930), 61.

40. This discussion is drawn from the Group for the Advancement of Psychiatry, *Us and Them: The Psychology of Ethnonationalism* (New York: Brunner/Mazel, 1987); Vamik Volkan, "Psychoanalytic Aspects of Ethnic Conflicts," in *Conflict and Peacemaking in Multiethnic Societies,* ed. J. V. Montville (Lexington, MA: Lexington Books, 1991); and Vamik Volkan, *The Need to Have Enemies and Allies: From Clinical Practice to International Relationships* (Northvale, NJ: Aronson, 1994).

41. Volkan, 1994.

42. Volkan has done this in his study of Cyprus, and some of those concepts will be discussed in the next chapter. Vamik Volkan, *Cyprus—War and Adaptation: A Psychoanalytic History of Two Ethnic Groups in Conflict* (Charlottesville: University Press of Virginia, 1979).

43. This view is most commonly associated with Konrad Lorenz and Robert Ardrey. See Konrad Lorenz, *On Aggression,* trans. M. K. Wilson (New York: Harcourt, Brace & World, 1966); and Robert Ardrey, *The Territorial Imperative: A Personal Inquiry into the Animal Origins of Property and Nations* (New York: Athenaeum, 1966).

44. R. Paul Shaw and Yuwa Wong, *Genetic Seeds of Warfare: Evolution, Nationalism, and Patriotism* (Boston: Unwin Hyman, 1989), 7.

45. Jeffrey H. Goldstein, "Beliefs about Human Aggression," in J. Groebel and R. A. Hinde, eds., *Aggression and War: Their Biological and Social Bases* (Cambridge: Cambridge University Press, 1989).

46. See Erich Fromm, *The Anatomy of Human Destructiveness* (New York: Henry Holt & Company, 1973), for a review.

47. Neil. R. Carlson, *Physiology of Behavior,* 7th ed. (Boston: Allyn & Bacon, 2001), 361-369.

48. Diane McGuiness, "Introduction: The Function of Status and Rank in Inter-Male Aggression and War," in *Dominance, Aggression, and War,* ed. D. McGuiness (New York: Paragon House Publishers, 1987), xi.

49. Robert. A. Hinde and Jo Groebel, "The Problem of Aggression," in *Aggression and War: Their Biological and Social Bases,* ed. J. Groebel and R. A. Hinde (Cambridge: Cambridge University Press, 1989), 5.

50. Leonard Berkowitz, "Biological Roots: Are Humans Inherently Violent?" in B. Glad, ed., *Psychological Dimensions of War* (Newbury Park, CA: Sage Publications, 1989).

51. A recent analysis of this research can be found in Leonard Berkowitz, "Frustration-Aggression Hypothesis: Examination and Reformulation," *Psychological Bulletin* 106 (1989): 59-73.

52. Shaw and Wong, 1989.

53. Kenneth E. Moyer, "The Biological Basis of Dominance and Aggression," in *Dominance, Aggression, and War,* ed. D. McGuiness (New York: Paragon House Publishers, 1987).

54. This review comes from Allan Mazur and Alan Booth, "Testosterone and Dominance in Men," *Behavioral and Brain Sciences* 21 (1998): 353-397.

Chapter Three

1. Embassy of the Republic of Armenia, "Armenia: An Emerging Democracy" (Washington, D.C.: Embassy of the Republic of Armenia, n. d.), 1.

2. See Henri Tajfel, *Human Groups and Social Categories: Studies in Social Psychology* (Cambridge, U.K.: Cambridge University Press, 1981); and Henri Tajfel and John C. Turner, "The Social Identity Theory of Intergroup Behavior," in *Psychology of Intergroup Relations,* ed. S. Worschel and W.G. Austin (Chicago: Nelson-Hall Publishers, 1986).

3. For example, John C. Turner, Penelope J. Oakes, S. Alexander Haslam, and Craig McGarty, "Self and Collective: Cognition and Social Context," *Personality and Social Psychology Bulletin* 20 (1994): 454-463.

4. Anthony D. Smith, *National Identity* (London: Penguin Books, 1991), 14.

5. Benedict Anderson, *Imagined Communities: Reflections on the Origin and Spread of Nationalism* (London: Verso, 1983), 15.

6. See James V. Wertsch, "Narrative Tools of History and Identity," *Culture & Psychology* 3 (1997): 5-20, for an overview of recent scholarship in this area.

7. Richard Gombrich, *Theravada Buddhism: A Social History from Ancient Benares to Modern Colombo* (London: Routledge, 1988), 138.

8. *The Mahavamsa; or, The Great Chronicle of Ceylon,* trans. W. Geiger (London: Pali Text Society, 1980), chapter VII, verses 3-4.

9. Tessa Bartholomeusz and Chandra R. de Silva, "Buddhist Fundamentalism and Identity in Sri Lanka," in *Buddhist Fundamentalism and Minority Identities in Sri Lanka,* ed. T. J. Bartholomeusz and C. R. de Silva (Albany, NY: State University of New York Press, 1998).

10. For example, *Mahavamsa,* chapter XXV.

11. *Mahavamsa,* chapter XXV, verses 109-111.

12. Gannath Obeyesekere, "Sinhalese-Buddhist Identity in Ceylon," in *Ethnic Identity: Cultural Continuities and Change,* ed. G. de Vos and L. Romanucci-Ross (Palo Alto, CA: Mayfield Publishing Company, 1988), 234-235.

13. Peeter Tulviste, "History Taught at School Versus History Discovered at Home: The Case of Estonia," *European Journal of Psychology of Education* 9 (1994): 121-126.

14. "Chronology of Historical Events in Sri Lanka Together With Events in Jaffna from a Tamil Perspective," Web page available at: http://ourworld. compuserve.com/homepages/umberto/chronolo.htm, accessed December 7, 2000.

15. "History of Tamil Eelam: Early History," Web page available at http:// www.eelamweb.com/history/, accessed December 7, 2000.

16. Hugh Trevor-Roper, "The Invention of Tradition: The Highland Tradition of Scotland," in E. Hobsbawm and T. Ranger, eds., *The Invention of Tradition* (Cambridge: Cambridge University Press, 1992), 21-22.

17. "The Uses and Abuses of History," *The Economist* (21 December 1996): 71-74, gives a wide range of examples.

18. See Arie Vaserman and Rami Ginat, "National, Territorial or Religious Conflict? The Case of Nagorno-Karabakh," *Studies in Conflict and Terrorism* 17 (1994): 345-362, for an overview.

19. James V. Werstch, *Voices of Collective Remembering* (Cambridge: Cambridge University Press, 2001), especially chapter 4.

20. See Vilho Harle, *The Enemy With a Thousand Faces: The Tradition of the Other in Western Political Thought and History* (New York: Praeger, 2000), for a discussion.

21. See Bruce Matthews, "Sinhala Cultural and Buddhist Patriotic Organizations in Contemporary Sri Lanka," *Pacific Affairs* 61 (1988): 620-632, for a review of these explanations.

22. Gombrich, 1988, 23-31.

23. David Little, *Sri Lanka: The Invention of Enmity* (Washington, D.C.: United States Institute of Peace Press, 1994), 17.

24. Marshall R. Singer, "Prospects for Conflict Management in the Sri Lankan Ethnic Crisis," in *Conflict and Peacemaking in Multiethnic Societies,* ed. J. M. Montville (Lexington, MA: Lexington Books, 1991), 261.

25. Obeyesekere, 1988, and Little, 1994.

26. Ronald Grigor Suny, *Looking Toward Ararat: Armenia in Modern History* (Bloomington: Indiana University Press; 1993), chapter 1.

27. See Yo'av Karny, *Highlanders: A Journey to the Caucasus in Quest of Memory* (New York: Farrar, Straus, and Giroux, 2000), 374-403, for a complete presentation of this story.

28. Mark A. Freeman, "Linking Self and Social Structure: A Psychological Perspective on Social Identity in Sri Lanka," *Journal of Cross-Cultural Psychology* 32 (2001): 291-308.

29. Michael Billig, *Banal Nationalism* (Thousand Oaks, CA: Sage, 1995), 1-2.

30. See Anthony D. Smith, *The Ethnic Origins of Nations* (Oxford: Basil Blackwell, 1986), chapter 1, for a discussion.

31. See Harle, 2000, for a discussion.

32. For an extensive discussion of this point, see Billig, 1995.

33. See Ivo Andric, *The Bridge on the Drina,* trans. L. F. Edwards (Chicago: The University of Chicago Press, 1977; original work published 1945), for a fic-

tional account of this process over the course of 300 years in a Bosnian town.

34. Turner et al., 1994.

35. See John C. Turner, "Social Comparison and Social Identity: Some Prospects for Intergroup Behaviour," *European Journal of Social Psychology* 5 (1975): 5-34, for a clear statement of this position.

36. See Henri Tajfel, *Human Groups and Social Categories: Studies in Social Psychology* (Cambridge: Cambridge University Press, 1981), chapter 13, for a review of this research.

37. See Chester A. Insko, John Schopler, James F. Kennedy, Kenneth R. Dahl, Kenneth A. Graetz, and Stephen M. Drigotas, "Individual-Group Discontinuity from the Differing Perspectives of Campbell's Realistic Group Conflict Theory and Tajfel and Turner's Social Identity Theory," *Social Psychology Quarterly* 55 (1992): 272-291, for an elaboration of this approach.

38. Turner, 1975, p. 117.

39. Herbert C. Kelman, "Nationalism, Patriotism, and National Identity: Social-Psychological Dimensions," in *Patriotism: In the Lives of Individuals and Nations,* ed. D. Bar-Tal and E. Staub (Chicago: Nelson-Hall Publishers, 1997).

40. Liberation Tigers of Tamil Eelam, "Tamil Eelam Home Page," Web page available at http://eelam.com/tamil_eelam.html, accessed January 26, 2001.

41. Michael Specter, "Zhirinovsky and the Motherland," *The New York Times Magazine* (June 19, 1994): 28-56.

42. Peter R. Grant, "Ethnocentrism in Response to a Threat to Social Identity," *Journal of Social Behavior and Personality* 8 (1993): 143-154.

43. The seminal work in this areas is Leon Festinger, "A Theory of Social Comparison Processes," *Human Relations* 7 (1954): 117-140. It is further elaborated in Turner, 1975.

Chapter Four

1. See Harry C. Triandis, *Individualism and Collectivism* (Boulder, CO: Westview Press, 1995), for a review of the individualism-collectivism literature.

2. Roy F. Baumeister, *Identity: Cultural Change and the Struggle for Self* (New York: Oxford University Press, 1986), especially pp. 83–84; Roy F. Baumeister, "How the Self Became a Problem: A Psychological Review of Historical Research," *Journal of Personality and Social Psychology* 52 (1987): 163-176; Roy F. Baumeister, *Escaping the Self: Alcoholism, Spirituality, Masochism, and Other Flights from the Burden of Selfhood* (New York: Basic Books, 1991).

3. An example is Matthew McKay, Patrick Fanning, Carole Honeychurch, and Catharine Sutker, *The Self-Esteem Companion: Simple Exercises to Help You Challenge Your Inner Critic and Celebrate Your Personal Strengths* (Oakland, CA: New Harbinger Publications, Inc., 1999).

4. Jack Canfield and Harold C. Wells, *100 Ways to Enhance Self-Concept in the Classroom: A Handbook for Teachers and Parents* (Englewood Cliffs, NJ: Prentice-Hall, 1976), is an early example.

5. Maureen Stout, *The Feel-Good Curriculum: The Dumbing-Down of America's Kids in the Name of Self-Esteem* (Cambridge, MA: Perseus Books, 2000).

6. Clifford Geertz, "From the Native's Point of View: On the Nature of Anthropological Understanding," in *Culture Theory: Essays on Mind, Self, and Emotion,* ed. R. A. Shweder and R. A. LeVine, (Cambridge: Cambridge University Press, 1984). See also Triandis, 1995.

7. Richard A. Shweder and E. J. Bourne, "Does the Concept of the Person Vary Cross-Culturally?" in *Culture Theory: Essays on Mind, Self, and Emotion,* ed. R. A. Shweder and R. A. LeVine (Cambridge: Cambridge University Press, 1984).

8. Baumeister, 1987.

9. Rupert Gethin, *The Foundations of Buddhism* (Oxford: Oxford University Press, 1998), 133.

10. The general outline of this example is drawn from Henepola Gunaratana, *Mindfulness in Plain English* (Boston: Wisdom Publications, 1993).

11. Walpola Sri Rahula, *What the Buddha Taught,* rev. ed. (New York: Grove Press, 1974), 55.

12. Paul Tillich, *The Courage to Be* (New Haven: Yale University Press, 1952), 42–45.

13. See Library of Congress, "Israel—A Country Study," for a discussion of the issue of "Who Is a Jew?" Available via the Web at: http://lcweb2.loc.gov/frd/cs/iltoc.html, accessed December 21, 2000.

14. F. James Davis, *Who Is Black? One Nation's Definition* (University Park, PA: The Pennsylvania State University Press, 1991), 8–11.

15. Glynis M. Breakwell, *Coping with Threatened Identities* (London: Methuen, 1986), 71–75.

16. Encyclopædia Britannica Online, "Armenian massacres," Web page available at http://search.eb.com/bol/topic?eu=9633&sctn=1, accessed December 26, 2000.

17. Ronald Grigor Suny, *The Revenge of the Past: Nationalism, Revolution, and the Collapse of the Soviet Union* (Stanford, CA: Stanford University Press, 1993), 74.

18. Ronald Grigor Suny, *Looking Toward Ararat: Armenia in Modern History* (Bloomington: Indiana University Press; 1993), 11.

19. Suny, 1993, 3.

20. Sihala Urumaya, "Now or Never—The Last Battle, If You Don't Act This Instant!" Web page available at http://sihalaurumaya.s5.com/plsread.htm, accessed January 27, 2001.

21. Lutz Oette, *The International Crime of Genocide: The Case of the Tamil People in Sri Lanka* (London: Tamil Information Centre, 1997).

22. Stanley J. Tambiah, *Sri Lanka: Ethnic Fratricide and the Dismantling of Democracy* (Chicago: The University of Chicago Press, 1986), 19-20.

23. See, for example, "Destruction of Jaffna Public Library," Web page published by TamilCanadian.com., available at: http://www.tamilcanadian.com/eelam/hrights/html/article/SU980516114546N30.html, accessed December 27, 2000; and Oette, 1997, 23.

24. Montreal Gazette (editorial), "Legal in English," 22 June 2000, sec. B, p. 2.

25. Mordecai Richler, *Oh Canada! Oh Quebec!: Requiem for a Divided Country* (New York: A. A. Knopf, 1992), chapter 1.

26. Sean Gordon, Mike King, and David Johnston, "Café Attacks Deplored: The Extremists Who Firebombed Three Second Cup Outlets in Montreal Have Forgotten the Painful Lessons of the October Crisis, Public Security Minister Serge Menard Says," *Montreal Gazette,* 7 October 2000, sec. A, p. 1.

27. Montreal Gazette (editorial), "Language and Sovereignty," 9 May 2000, sec. B, p. 2.

28. Zori Balayan, *Between Heaven and Hell: The Struggle for Karabakh,* trans. by Marite Sapiets, Michael Rowe, and Felix Corley (Yerevan: Amaras Publishers, 1997; original work published 1995), 17.

29. For a comprehensive statement of this approach, see "Lecture XXXII" in Sigmund Freud, *New Introductory Lectures on Psychoanalysis,* trans. and ed. J. Strachey (New York: W.W. Norton & Co., 1964; original work published 1933).

30. Erich Neumann, *Depth Psychology and a New Ethic,* trans. E. Rolfe (New York: G.P. Putnam's Sons, 1969; original work published 1949), 79.

31. Abraham H. Maslow, *Toward a Psychology of Being,* 2nd ed. (New York: D. Van Nostrand Company, 1968), 5.

32. Carl R. Rogers, *The Carl Rogers Reader,* ed. H. Kirschenbaum and V. L. Henderson (Boston: Houghton Mifflin Company, 1989), chapter 17.

33. See Neumann, 1969, chapter 2.

34. Genesis, chapter 3, Revised Standard Version.

35. Romans 5:12, Revised Standard Version.

36. Susan L. Nelson, *Healing the Broken Heart: Sin, Alienation, and the Gift of Grace* (St. Louis: Chalice Press, 1997), chapter 3.

37. Paul Tillich, *The Shaking of the Foundations* (New York, C. Scribner's Sons, 1950); see especially the sermon titled "You Are Accepted."

38. Romans 7:13-20.

39. Jesuit Scholars, *Religious Hinduism* (Bombay: St. Paul Publications, 1964), chapter 11.

40. Deuteronomy 14:3-8.

41. Mary Douglas, *Purity and Danger: An Analysis of the Concepts of Pollution and Taboo* (New York: Praeger Publishers, 1966), 34.

42. See Imam Ali Foundation, "Islamic Laws," Web site available at http://www.najaf.org/English/law/, accessed December 27, 2000, for a description.

43. Ed Harper, cited in Douglas, 1966, 9.

44. For one collection, see James Morgan Read, *Atrocity Propaganda 1914-1919* (New Haven: Yale University Press, 1941).

45. Lance Morrow, "Unspeakable Crimes," *Time* (February 22, 1993): 48-50.

46. Shana Swiss, Peggy J. Jennings, Gladys V. Aryee, Grace H. Brown, Ruth M. Jappah-Samukai, Mary S. Kamara, Rosana D. H. Schaack, and Rujatu S. Turay-Kanneh, "Violence Against Women During the Liberian Civil Conflict (Letter from Monrovia)," *JAMA, The Journal of the American Medical Association* 279 (February 25, 1998): 625-630.

47. Human Rights Watch, "World Report 1999: Women's Human Rights—Violence Against Women," Web page available at http://www.hrw.org/hrw/worldreport99/women/women2.html, accessed January 29, 2001.

48. "Rwanda: Genocidal Rape Conviction," *Off Our Backs* 29 (1999): 4.

49. Morrow, 1993, 49.

50. Michael C. Adams, *The Great Adventure: Male Desire and the Coming of World War I* (Bloomington, IN: Indiana University Press, 1990).

51. Ernest Becker, *Escape from Evil* (New York: Free Press, 1973), 115-116.

52. Quoted in Barry Bearak, "A Jihad Leader Finds the U.S. Perplexingly Fickle," *The New York Times,* October 10, 2000: sec. A, p. 3.

53. Ervin Staub, *The Roots of Evil: The Origins of Genocide and Other Group Violence* (Cambridge, U.K.: Cambridge University Press, 1989), 192.

54. Robert Conquest, *The Great Terror: A Reassessment* (New York: Oxford University Press, 1990), 486.

55. Madison Grant, *The Passing of the Great Race* (New York: Charles Scribner's Sons, 1916), 49.

56. See, for example, "Erasing History: Ethnic Cleansing in Kosovo," report released by the U.S. Department of State, Washington, D.C., May 1999. Available via the Web at http://www.state.gov/www/regions/eur/rpt_9905_ethnic_ksvo_toc.html, accessed December 28, 2000.

Chapter Five

1. Levon Ter-Petrossian, in a speech in 1996, when he was the President of Armenia. Quoted in Yo'av Karny, *Highlanders: A Journey to the Caucasus in Quest of Memory* (New York: Farrar, Straus, and Giroux, 2000), 396.

2. This material is taken from an interview with a member of Artsakh Hayastan, an organization dedicated to achieving a peaceful solution to the "Karabakh question," in Yerevan, May 31, 2000.

3. Arie Vaserman, and Rami Ginat, "National, Territorial or Religious Conflict? The Case of Nagorno-Karabakh," *Studies in Conflict and Terrorism* 17 (1994): 345-362, especially 347.

4. Karny, 2000, 389.

5. Zori Balayan, *Between Heaven and Hell: The Struggle for Karabakh,* trans. M. Sapiets, M. Rowe, and F. Corley (Yerevan: Amaras Publishers, 1997; original work published 1995), 453.

6. These comments are drawn from my interviews with a variety of Azerbaijani refugees in Baku and surrounding areas, May 25-29, 2000.

7. For an extensive review of the Azerbaijani position on this history, see Embassy of the Republic of Azerbaijan in the United States, "Armenian-Azerbaijani Conflict: Background," Web page available at http://www.azembassy.com/confl/confl_backgr.html, accessed January 3, 2001.

8. Vaserman and Ginat, 1994, 348.

9. Karny, 2000, 374-381.

10. Vaserman and Ginat, 1994, 349.

11. Juliet O'Neill, "No Massacre Took Place, Armenia says; Victims Were Used as Cover During Fight, Authorities Say," *The Vancouver Sun,* 6 March 1992, sec. A, p. 10.

12. Vafa Guluzade, "Karabakh: The Armenia-Azerbaijan Conflict," *Azerbaijan International* 6 (1998). Available via the Web at http://azer.com/aiweb/categories/magazine/62_folder/62_articles/62_karabakh.html, accessed January 3, 2001.

13. Liberation Tigers of Tamil Eelam, "The Legitimacy of the Armed Struggle of the Tamil People," Web page available at http://eelam.com/introduction/legitimacy.html, accessed January 3, 2001.

14. The Office of Tibet in London, "Tibet: Proving Truth from Facts," Web site available at http://www.tibet.com/WhitePaper/index.html, accessed January 3, 2001.

15. Bagrat Shinkwba, et al., "Appeal to the Russian Writers' Union, Writers' Organisations of the CIS States, the North Caucasian Republics, Tataria, Bashkortostan, Near Eastern Countries: Lebanon, Syria, Jordan, Egypt; of America, Turkey, England, Germany, France, Poland, Czech Republic, Hungary, Baltic Republics and other States," Web page available at http://www.abkhazia.org/writers.html, accessed January 3, 2001.

16. Gouvernement du Québec, "Political and Constitutional Status," document available at the official Web site of the Prime Minister of Quebec, at http://www.premier.gouv.qc.ca/premier_ministre/english/major_issues/index_politique.html, accessed January 3, 2001.

17. Balayan, 1997, 16.

18. Michael Adams describes how Middle Ages imagery was used by soldiers in the Civil War and World War I to ease their participation in it. Michael C. Adams, *The Great Adventure: Male Desire and the Coming of World War I* (Bloomington: Indiana University Press, 1990).

19. See John E. Mack, "Nationalism and the Self," *The Psychohistory Review* 11(1983): 47-69, for a discussion.

20. For a brief description of Black January, see Michael P. Croissant, *The Armenia-Azerbaijan Conflict: Causes and Implications* (Westport, CT: Praeger, 1998), 37. A personal description by a woman who lost a daughter in the fighting can be found at Galina Mammadova, "Larissa/Black January—January 20, 1990," *Azerbaijan International* 7 (Autumn 1999).

21. Ronald Grigor Suny, *Looking Toward Ararat: Armenia in Modern History* (Bloomington: Indiana University Press; 1993), 228.
22. See Vamik Volkan, *The Need to Have Enemies and Allies: From Clinical Practice to International Relationships* (Northvale, NJ: Jason Aronson, 1994), 169-172, for a discussion of the psychological role of monuments and memorials.
23. Ian Buruma, "The Joys and Perils of Victimhood," *The New York Review of Books* 46 (April 8, 1999): 4-9.
24. Neil Renwick and Qing Cao, "China's Political Discourse Towards the 21st Century: Victimhood, Identity, and Political Power," *East Asia: An International Quarterly* 17 (1999), 111ff.
25. Links to all of these resolutions can be found at Armenian National Institute, "International Affirmation of the Armenian Genocide," Web site available at http://www.armenian-genocide.org/affirmation/affirmintro.htm#resolutions, accessed January 4, 2001.
26. APCO Associates, Inc., "Lost Generation: Section 907 and the Refugees in Azerbaijan," videotape featuring the Honorary Lawrence S. Eagleburger, produced with a grant from Frontera Resources Corporation, n. d.
27. See, for example, the TamilCanadian Web site at http://www.tamilcanadian.com/ and the official LTTE Web site at http://www.eelam.com.
28. See, for example, National Movement Against Terrorism, "The Gonagala Massacre by the LTTE" (Colombo: National Movement Against Terrorism, n. d.). This 12-page booklet contains graphic photographs of an alleged massacre of Sinhalese civilians.
29. Mack, 1983, 61-63.
30. John E. Mack, "Foreword," in V. Volkan, *Cyprus—War and Adaptation: A Psychoanalytic History of Two Ethnic Groups in Conflict* (Charlottesville, VA: University Press of Virginia, 1979), xvi.
31. Sangam Research U.S.A., "Kosovo (before NATO) and Tamil Eelam," (1999). Pamphlet available from Ilankai Tamil Sangam at the e-mail address: secretary@sangam.org
32. See Buruma, 1999, for a discussion.
33. This discussion is greatly influenced by Fritz Heider, *The Psychology of Interpersonal Relations* (New York: John Wiley & Sons, 1958), 265-270.
34. Stanley J. Tambiah, *Sri Lanka: Ethnic Fratricide and the Dismantling of Democracy* (Chicago: The University of Chicago Press, 1986), 16.
35. See Dean G. Pruitt and Jeffrey Z. Rubin, *Social Conflict: Escalation, Stalemate, and Settlement* (New York: Random House, 1986), for an extended discussion of escalation in conflict.
36. Seneca, *Thyestes* (American Philological Association Textbook Series #11), ed. R. J. Tarrant (Atlanta: Oxford University Press, 1985), 195-196.
37. Sung Hee Kim and Richard H. Smith, "Revenge and Conflict Escalation," *Negotiation Journal* 9 (1993): 37-43.

38. Canadian Press Newswire, "Israelis Rocket Palestinian Targets in Gaza in Revenge for Bus Attack," November 20, 2000, sec. N.

39. Roy F. Baumeister and W. Keith Campbell, "The Intrinsic Appeal of Evil: Sadism, Sensational Thrills, and Threatened Egotism," *Personality and Social Psychology Review* 3 (1999): 210-221.

40. Quoted in Ernest Becker, *Escape from Evil* (New York: Free Press, 1973), 115.

41. Erich Fromm, *The Anatomy of Human Destructiveness* (New York: Henry Holt & Company, 1973), 259-260.

42. Fromm, 1973, 261.

43. See Erik H. Erikson, *Identity: Youth and Crisis* (New York: W.W. Norton & Company, 1968), for an extensive discussion.

44. Ervin Staub, *The Roots of Evil: The Origins of Genocide and Other Group Violence* (Cambridge, U.K.: Cambridge University Press, 1989).

45. Rollo May, *Man's Search for Himself* (New York: W. W. Norton & Company, Inc., 1953).

46. Victor A. Shnirelman, *Who Gets the Past? Competition for Ancestors Among Non-Russian Intellectuals in Russia* (Washington, D.C.: The Woodrow Wilson Center Press, 1996).

47. Vilho Harle, *The Enemy With a Thousand Faces: The Tradition of the Other in Western Political Thought and History* (New York: Praeger, 2000).

48. I have changed the names, but the details of Arman's life are accurate, as reported by his parents.

Chapter Six

1. See Kumar Rupesinghe, ed., *Negotiating Peace in Sri Lanka: Efforts, Failures, and Lessons* (London: International Alert, 1998), for descriptions of these negotiations.

2. I have changed the names of the students, but all other details of this interaction are accurate.

3. This is a reference to my having penalized them later for using force to achieve their task.

4. Jane Perlez and David E. Sanger, "White House Says It Sees Some Hope to End Standoff," *The New York Times,* April 6, 2001, sec. A, p. 1.

5. Craig S. Smith, "U.S. and China Look for a Way to Say 'Sorry': Right Apology Depends on Its Interpretation," *The New York Times,* April 9, 2001, sec. A, p. 1.

6. Craig S. Smith, "China Releases U.S. Plane Crew 11 Days After Midair Collision: Envoy 'Very Sorry,'" *The New York Times,* April 12, 2001, sec. A., p. 1.

7. See Ronald J. Fisher, *Interactive Conflict Resolution* (Syracuse, NY: Syracuse University Press, 1997), for an overview.

8. Max M. Kampelman, "Remarks by Max M. Kampelman at the 25th Anniversary Conference of the Society of Professionals in Dispute Resolution," Web page available at http://www.usip.org/oc/pubs/MKSpeech1.html, accessed February 2, 2001.

9. Timothy D. Sisk, ed., *New Approaches to International Negotiation and Mediation: Findings from USIP-Sponsored Research* (Washington, D.C.: United States Institute of Peace, 1999), 3.

10. The LTTE leader's last name is also sometimes transliterated as "Prabhakaran" and "Pirapaharan."

11. Anton Balasingham, *The Politics of Duplicity: Revisiting the Jaffna Talks* (Mitcham, U.K.: Fairmax Publishing, Ltd., 2000), 20.

12. P. Rajanayagam, "Government–LTTE Negotiations (1994-1995): Another Lost Opportunity," in K. Rupesinghe, ed., *Negotiating Peace in Sri Lanka: Efforts, Failures, and Lessons* (London: International Alert, 1998).

13. Balasingham, 2000, 146.

14. See "Sihala Urumaya to Help Crush Terrorism," Web page available at: http://sihalaurumaya.s5.com/SUto%20crush.htm, for a version of this argument.

15. Quoted in Jehan Perera, "An Analysis of the Breakdown of Negotiations in the Sri Lankan Ethnic Conflict," in K. Rupesinghe (ed.), 1998, 245. Perera makes similar points about the nature of identity in his discussion of the talks.

16. Velupillai Pirabakaran, "2000 Heroes' Day Message," posted as a press release by Eelam House in London. Available via the Web at http://eelam.com/freedom_struggle/ltte_press_releases/2000/november/27.html, November 29, 2000.

17. This organization was called "The Conference on Security and Cooperation in Europe" (CSCE) before December 1994.

18. Michael P. Croissant, *The Armenia-Azerbaijan Conflict: Causes and Implications* (Westport, CT: Praeger, 1998), 121.

19. Max Kampelman, "Secession and the Right of Self-Determination: An Urgent Need to Harmonize Principle with Pragmatism," *The Washington Quarterly* (Summer 1993): 5-12.

20. See Herbert C. Kelman, "Acknowledging the Other's Nationhood: How to Create a Momentum for the Israeli-Palestinian Negotiations," *Journal of Palestine Studies* 85 (1992): 18-38.

21. Herbert C. Kelman, "Nationalism, Patriotism, and National Identity: Social-Psychological Dimensions," in *Patriotism: In the Lives of Individuals and Nations,* ed. D. Bar-Tal and E. Staub (Chicago: Nelson-Hall Publishers, 1997).

22. Herbert C. Kelman, "Negotiating National Identity and Self-Determination in Ethnic Conflicts: The Choice Between Pluralism and Ethnic Cleansing," *Negotiation Journal* 13: 327-340.

23. Robert N. Kearney, "Territorial Elements of Tamil Separatism in Sri Lanka," *Pacific Affairs* 60 (1988): 561-567.
24. Chelvadurai Manogaran, "Space-Related Identity in Sri Lanka," in D. H. Kaplan and G. H. Herb, eds., *Nested Identities: Nationalism, Territory, and Scale* (Lanham, MD: Rowman & Littlefield Publishers, Inc., 1999).
25. Amita Shastri, "The Material Basis for Separatism: The Tamil Eelam Movement in Sri Lanka," *The Journal of Asian Studies* 49 (1990): 56-77.
26. "The legitimacy of the armed struggle of the Tamil people," Web page produced by Eelam House in London, available via the Web at: http://eelam.com/introduction/legitimacy.html, accessed January 22, 2001.
27. International Alert, *Sri Lanka: Negotiations, Agreements and Statements of Principle of the Sri Lankan Government and Tamil Parties* (London: International Alert, 1994), iv.
28. Pirabakaran, 2000.
29. Patricia Carley, *Nagorno-Karabakh: Searching for a Solution* (A United States Institute of Peace Roundtable Report) (Washington, D.C.: United States Institute of Peace, 1998), 22.
30. For vivid descriptions of Nakhchivan and the feeling of Azerbaijanis for it, see Thomas Goltz, *Azerbaijan Diary: A Rogue Reporter's Adventures in an Oil-Rich, War-Torn, Post-Soviet Republic* (Armonk, NY: M. E. Sharpe, 1999).
31. See Herbert C. Kelman, "Social-Psychological Contributions to Peacemaking and Peacebuilding in the Middle East," *Applied Psychology: An International Review* 47 (1998): 5-28, for a description.
32. Joseph V. Montville, "The Healing Function in Political Conflict Resolution," in D. J. D. Sandole and H. van der Merwe, eds., *Conflict Resolution Theory and Practice: Integration and Application* (Manchester: Manchester University Press, 1993), 115.
33. Michael Ingatieff, "How Can Past Sins Be Absolved?" *World Press Review* 44 (1997, February): 6-9.
34. For example, see "Indictment Against Sri Lanka," Web page posted by Tamilnation. Available at http://www.tamilnation.org/indictment/indict04.htm; accessed January 22, 2001.
35. International Alert, 1994.
36. See Elazar Barkan, *The Guilt of Nations: Restitution and Negotiating Historical Injustices* (New York: Norton, 2000), for an extensive discussion of this issue.
37. Christian Caryl, "After a Half Century, an Apology Exchange," *U.S. News & World Report* 121 (Dec 23, 1996): 14.
38. See Robert A. Baruch Bush and Joseph P. Folger, *The Promise of Mediation: Responding to Conflict through Empowerment and Recognition* (San Francisco: Jossey-Bass, 1994), for one example.
39. For a discussion, see Joseph P. Folger, Marshall Scott Poole, and Randall K. Stutman, *Working Through Conflict: Strategies for Relationships, Groups, and Organizations,* 3rd ed. (New York: Longman, 1997), 129.

40. Susan Heitler, *The Power of Two: Secrets to a Strong & Loving Marriage* (Oakland, CA: New Harbinger Publications, 1997).

41. This idea was popularized in particular by Roger Fisher and William Ury, *Getting to Yes: Negotiating Agreement Without Giving In* (Boston: Houghton Mifflin, 1981).

42. See Amitai Etzioni, "The Evils of Self-Determination," *Foreign Policy* 89 (Winter 1992-1993): 21-35, for one discussion.

Chapter Seven

1. Paul Tillich, *The Shaking of the Foundations* (New York: C. Scribner's Sons, 1950), 157-158.

REFERENCES CITED

Adams, Michael C. *The Great Adventure: Male Desire and the Coming of World War I.* Bloomington, IN: Indiana University Press, 1990.

Adorno, Theodore W., Else Frenkel-Brunswick, Daniel J. Levinson, and R. Nevitt Sanford. *The Authoritarian Personality.* New York: Harper & Row, 1950.

Allport, Gordon W. *The Nature of Prejudice.* Garden City, NJ: Doubleday, 1954.

Allport, Gordon W., and Leo Postman. *The Psychology of Rumor.* New York: Henry Holt & Company, 1946.

Altemeyer, Bob. *The Authoritarian Specter.* Cambridge, MA: Harvard University Press, 1996.

Amnesty International. "Sri Lanka: Amnesty International Report 2000." Annual human rights report. London: Amnesty International Publications, 2000.

Anderson, Benedict. *Imagined Communities: Reflections on the Origin and Spread of Nationalism.* London: Verso, 1983.

Andric, Ivo. *The Bridge on the Drina.* Translated from the Serbo-Croat by L. F. Edwards. Chicago: The University of Chicago Press, 1977 (original work published 1945).

APCO Associates, Inc. "Lost Generation: Section 907 and the Refugees in Azerbaijan." Videotape featuring the Honorary Lawrence S. Eagleburger. Produced with a grant from Frontera Resources Corporation, no date.

Ardrey, Robert. *The Territorial Imperative: A Personal Inquiry into the Animal Origins of Property and Nations.* New York: Atheneum, 1966.

Armenian National Institute. "International Affirmation of the Armenian Genocide." Web site available at http://www.armenian-genocide.org/affirmation/affirmintro.htm#resolutions. Accessed January 4, 2001.

Associated Press. "Sri Lankan Mob Kills 25 Hostage-Takers." *The Toronto Star* (26 October 2000): News Section.

Balasingham, Anton. *The Politics of Duplicity: Revisiting the Jaffna Talks.* Mitcham, U.K.: Fairmax Publishing, Ltd., 2000.

Balayan, Zori. *Between Heaven and Hell: The Struggle for Karabakh.* Translated by Marite Sapiets, Michael Rowe, and Felix Corley. Yerevan: Amaras Publishers, 1997 (original work published 1995).

Barkan, Elazar. *The Guilt of Nations: Restitution and Negotiating Historical Injustices.* New York: Norton, 2000.

Bartholomeusz, Tessa, and Chandra R. de Silva. "Buddhist Fundamentalism and Identity in Sri Lanka." In *Buddhist Fundamentalism and Minority Identities in Sri Lanka,* edited by T. J. Bartholomeusz and C. R. de Silva. Albany, NY: State University of New York Press, 1998.

Baumeister, Roy F. *Identity: Cultural Change and the Struggle for Self.* New York: Oxford University Press, 1986.

——— "How the Self Became a Problem: A Psychological Review of Historical Research." *Journal of Personality and Social Psychology* 52 (1987): 163-176.

——— *Escaping the Self: Alcoholism, Spirituality, Masochism, and Other Flights from the Burden of Selfhood.* New York: Basic Books, 1991.

Baumeister, Roy F., and W. Keith Campbell. "The Intrinsic Appeal of Evil: Sadism, Sensational Thrills, and Threatened Egotism." *Personality and Social Psychology Review* 3 (1999): 210-221.

Bearak, Barry. "A Jihad Leader Finds the U.S. Perplexingly Fickle." *The New York Times* (Tuesday, October 10, 2000): A3.

Becker, Ernest. *Escape from Evil.* New York: Free Press, 1973.

Berkowitz, Leonard. "Biological Roots: Are Humans Inherently Violent?" In Betty Glad, ed., *Psychological Dimensions of War.* Newbury Park, CA: Sage Publications, 1989.

——— "Frustration-Aggression Hypothesis: Examination and Reformulation." *Psychological Bulletin* 106 (1989), 59-73.

Billig, Michael. *Banal Nationalism.* Thousand Oaks, CA: Sage, 1995.

Blake, Robert R., and Jane S. Mouton. "From Theory to Practice in Interface Problem Solving." In S. Worschel and W. G. Austin, eds., *Psychology of Intergroup Relations.* Chicago: Nelson-Hall Publishers, 1986.

Breakwell, Glynis M. *Coping with Threatened Identities.* London: Methuen, 1986.

Brewer, Marilynn B. "Ingroup Bias in the Minimal Intergroup Situation: A Cognitive-Motivational Analysis." *Psychological Bulletin* 86 (1979), 307-324.

Brewer, Marilynn B., and Norman Miller. *Intergroup Relations.* Pacific Grove, CA: Brooks/Cole Publishing Company, 1996.

Buruma, Ian. "The Joys and Perils of Victimhood." *The New York Review of Books* 46 (April 8, 1999): 4-9.

Bush, Robert A. Baruch, and Joseph P. Folger. *The Promise of Mediation: Responding to Conflict Through Empowerment and Recognition.* San Francisco: Jossey-Bass, 1994.

Canfield, Jack, and Harold C. Wells. *100 Ways to Enhance Self-Concept in the Classroom: A Handbook for Teachers and Parents.* Englewood Cliffs, NJ: Prentice-Hall, 1976.

Carley, Patricia. *Nagorno-Karabakh: Searching for a Solution* (A United States Institute of Peace Roundtable Report). Washington, D.C.: United States Institute of Peace, 1998.

Carlson, Neil R. *Physiology of Behavior,* 7th ed. Boston: Allyn & Bacon, 2001.

Caryl, Christian. "After a Half Century, an Apology Exchange." *U.S. News & World Report* 121 (Dec 23, 1996): 14.

"Chronology of Historical Events in Sri Lanka Together with Events in Jaffna from a Tamil Perspective." Web page available at: http://ourworld.compuserve.com/homepages/umberto/chronolo.htm, accessed December 7, 2000.

Cohen, Claudia E. "Person Categories and Social Perception: Testing Some Boundaries of the Processing Effects of Prior Knowledge." *Journal of Social and Personality Psychology* 40 (1981): 441-452.

Conquest, Robert. *The Great Terror: A Reassessment.* New York: Oxford University Press, 1990.

Croissant, Michael P. *The Armenia-Azerbaijan Conflict: Causes and Implications.* Westport, CT: Praeger, 1998.

Davis, F. James. *Who Is Black? One Nation's Definition.* University Park, PA: Pennsylvania State University Press, 1991.

Dawes, Robyn M., David Singer, and Frank Lemons, "An Experimental Analysis of the Contrast Effect and its Implications for Intergroup Communication and the Indirect Assessment of Attitude." *Journal of Personality and Social Psychology* 21 (1972), 281.

"Death Toll in Ethnic Violence in Sri Lanka Revised to 362," *New York Times,* 11 August 1983, p. A6.

Doise, Willem. "An Experimental Investigation into the Formation of Intergroup Representations." *European Journal of Social Psychology* 2 (1972): 202-204.

Doob, Leonard W. *Patriotism and Nationalism: Their Psychological Foundations.* New Haven: Yale University Press, 1964.

Douglas, Mary. *Purity and Danger: An Analysis of the Concepts of Pollution and Taboo.* New York: Praeger Publishers, 1966.

Embassy of the Republic of Armenia in the U.S. "Armenia: An Emerging Democracy." Washington, D.C.: Embassy of the Republic of Armenia, no date.

Embassy of the Republic of Azerbaijan in the U.S. "Armenian-Azerbaijani Conflict: Background." Web page available at http://www.azembassy.com/confl/confl_backgr.html, accessed January 3, 2001.

Encyclopædia Britannica Online. "Armenian massacres." Web page available at http://search.eb.com/bol/topic?eu=9633&sctn=1, accessed December 26, 2000.

Erikson, Erik H. *Identity: Youth and Crisis.* New York: W.W. Norton & Company, 1968.

Etzioni, Amitai. "The Evils of Self-Determination." *Foreign Policy* 89 (Winter 1992-1993): 21-35.

Festinger, Leon. "A Theory of Social Comparison Processes." *Human Relations* 7 (1954): 117-140.

Festinger, Leon, Dorwin Cartright, Kathleen Barber, Juliet Fleischl, Josephine Gottsdanker, Annette Keysen, and Gloria Leavitt. "A Study of Rumor: Its Origin and Spread." *Human Relations* 1 (1948), 464-485.

Fisher, Ronald J. *Interactive Conflict Resolution.* Syracuse, NY: Syracuse University Press, 1997.

Folger, Joseph P., Marshall Scott Poole, and Randall K. Stutman. *Working Through Conflict: Strategies for Relationships, Groups, and Organizations,* 3rd ed. New York: Longman, 1997.

Forbes, Hugh Donald. *Nationalism, Ethnocentrism, and Personality.* Chicago: University of Chicago Press, 1985.

Forsyth, Donelson R. *Group Dynamics,* 3rd ed. Belmont, CA: Brooks/Cole-Wadsworth Publishing Company, 1999.

Freeman, Mark A. "Linking Self and Social Structure: A Psychological Perspective on Social Identity in Sri Lanka." *Journal of Cross-Cultural Psychology* 32 (2001): 291-308.

Freud, Sigmund. *Group Psychology and the Analysis of the Ego.* Translated and edited by James Strachey. New York: W.W. Norton & Co., 1959 (original work published 1922).

――― *Civilization and Its Discontents.* Translated by J. Strachey. New York: W. W. Norton & Co., 1961 (original work published 1930).

――― *New Introductory Lectures on Psychoanalysis.* Translated and edited by James Strachey. New York: W.W. Norton & Co., 1964 (original work published 1933).

Fromm, Erich. *Man for Himself: An Inquiry into the Psychology of Ethics.* New York: Rinehart and Company, Incorporated, 1947.

――― *The Anatomy of Human Destructiveness.* New York: Henry Holt & Company, 1973.

Gaibov, B., and A. Sharifov. *Undeclared War,* trans. Y. Rahimov. Baku: Communist Publishing House, 1991.

Geertz, Clifford. "From the Native's Point of View: On the Nature of Anthropological Understanding." In *Culture Theory: Essays on Mind, Self, and Emotion,* edited by R. A. Shweder and R. A. LeVine. Cambridge, U.K.: Cambridge University Press, 1984.

Gethin, Rupert. *The Foundations of Buddhism.* Oxford: Oxford University Press, 1998.

Gilovich, Thomas. "Seeing the Past in the Present: The Effects of Associations to Familiar Events on Judgments and Decisions." *Journal of Personality and Social Psychology* 40 (1981): 797-808.

Goldstein, Jeffrey H. "Beliefs about Human Aggression." In Jo Groebel and Robert A. Hinde (eds.), *Aggression and War: Their Biological and Social Bases. Cambridge,* U.K.: Cambridge University Press, 1989.

Goltz, Thomas. *Azerbaijan Diary : A Rogue Reporter's Adventures in an Oil-Rich, War-Torn, Post-Soviet Republic.* Armonk, NY: M. E. Sharpe, 1999.

Gombrich, Richard. *Theravada Buddhism: A Social History from Ancient Benares to Modern Colombo.* London: Routledge, 1988.

Gordon, Sean, Mike King, and David Johnston. "Café Attacks Deplored: The Extremists Who Firebombed Three Second Cup Outlets in Montreal Have Forgotten the Painful Lessons of the October Crisis, Public Security Minister Serge Menard Says." *Montreal Gazette,* October 7, 2000, section A, p. 1.

Gouvernement du Québec. "Political and Constitutional Status." Document available at the official Web site of the Prime Minister of Quebec, at http://www.premier.gouv.qc.ca/premier_ministre/english/major_issues/index_politique.html, accessed January 3, 2001.

Grant, Madison. *The Passing of the Great Race.* New York: Charles Scribner's Sons, 1916.

Grant, Peter R. "Ethnocentrism in Response to a Threat to Social Identity." *Journal of Social Behavior and Personality* 8 (1993): 143-154.

Group for the Advancement of Psychiatry. *Us and Them: The Psychology of Ethnonationalism.* New York: Brunner/Mazel, 1987.

Guluzade, Vafa. "Karabakh: The Armenia-Azerbaijan Conflict." *Azerbaijan International* 6 (1998). Available via the Web at http://azer.com/aiweb/categories/magazine/62_folder/62_articles/62_karabakh.html. Accessed January 3, 2001.

Gunaratana, Henepola. *Mindfulness in Plain English.* Boston: Wisdom Publications, 1992.

Gunaratna, Rohan. *International and Regional Security Implications of the Sri Lankan Tamil Insurgency.* St. Albans, U.K.: International Foundation of Sri Lankans, 1997.

Haney, Craig, Curtis Banks, and Philip Zimbardo. "Interpersonal Dynamics in a Simulated Prison." *International Journal of Criminology and Penology* 1 (1973): 69-97.

Harle, Vilho. *The Enemy With a Thousand Faces : The Tradition of the Other in Western Political Thought and History.* New York: Praeger, 2000.

Heider, Fritz. *The Psychology of Interpersonal Relations.* New York: John Wiley & Sons, 1958.

Heitler, Susan. *The Power of Two: Secrets to a Strong & Loving Marriage.* Oakland, CA: New Harbinger Publications, 1997.

"History of Tamil Eelam: Early History." Web page available at http://www.eelamweb.com/history/. Accessed December 7, 2000.

Hinde, Robert. A., and Jo Groebel. "The Problem of Aggression." In *Aggression and War: Their Biological and Social Bases,* edited by J. Groebel and R. A. Hinde. Cambridge, U.K.: Cambridge University Press, 1989.

Hollup, Oddvar. "The Impact of Land Reforms, Rural Images, and Nationalist Ideology on Plantation Tamils." In *Buddhist Fundamentalism and Minority Identities in Sri Lanka,* edited by T. A. Bartholomeusz and Chandra R. de Silva. Albany, NY: State University of New York Press, 1998.

Howard, John W., and Myron Rothbart. "Social Categorization for In-group and Out-group Behavior." *Journal of Social and Personality Psychology* 38 (1980): 301-310.

2   *References Cited*

2ibliography

Human Rights Watch. "World Report 1999: Women's Human Rights—Violence Against Women." Web page available at http://www.hrw.org/hrw/worldreport99/women/women2.html. Accessed January 29, 2001.

Imam Ali Foundation. "Islamic Laws." Web site available at http://www.najaf.org/English/law/. Accessed December 27, 2000.

Ingatieff, Michael. "How Can Past Sins Be Absolved?" *World Press Review* 44 (February, 1997): 6-9.

Insko, Chester A., John Schopler, James F. Kennedy, Kenneth R. Dahl, Kenneth A. Graetz, and Stephen M. Drigotas. "Individual-Group Discontinuity from the Differing Perspectives of Campbell's Realistic Group Conflict Theory and Tajfel and Turner's Social Identity Theory." *Social Psychology Quarterly* 55 (1992): 272-291.

International Alert. *Sri Lanka: Negotiations, Agreements and Statements of Principle of the Sri Lankan Government and Tamil Parties.* London: International Alert, 1994.

"Israelis Rocket Palestinian Targets in Gaza in Revenge for Bus Attack." *Canadian Press Newswire* (November 20, 2000): section N 20'00.

Jackson, Jay W. "Realistic Group Conflict Theory: A Review and Evaluation of the Theoretical and Empirical Literature." *The Psychological Record* 43 (1993): 395-414.

Jesuit Scholars. *Religious Hinduism.* Bombay: St. Paul Publications, 1964.

Judd, Charles M., and Judith M. Harackiewicz. "Contrast Effects in Attitude Judgment: An Examination of the Accentuation Hypothesis." *Journal of Personality and Social Psychology* 38 (1980), 390-398.

Judd, Charles M., and Bernadette Park. "Out-group Homogeneity: Judgments of Variability at the Individual and Group Levels." *Journal of Personality and Social Psychology* 54 (1988): 778-788.

Kampelman, Max. "Secession and the Right of Self-Determination: An Urgent Need to Harmonize Principle with Pragmatism." *The Washington Quarterly* (Summer 1993): 5-12.

Kampelman, Max M. "Remarks by Max M. Kampelman at the 25th Anniversary Conference of the Society of Professionals in Dispute Resolution," Web page available at http://www.usip.org/oc/pubs/MKSpeech1.html, accessed February 2, 2001.

Karny, Yo'av. *Highlanders: A Journey to the Caucasus in Quest of Memory.* New York: Farrar, Straus, and Giroux, 2000.

Karunatilake, Waruna. "Two dead as race riots worsen in Hill Country." *The Lanka Academic* (October 30, 2000). Accessible via the Web at http://www.lacnet.org/the_academic/archive/2000_10_30/

Kazemzadeh, Firuz. *The Struggle for Transcaucasia (1917-1921).* New York: Philosophical Library, Inc., 1951.

Kearney, Robert N. "Territorial Elements of Tamil Separatism in Sri Lanka." *Pacific Affairs* 60 (1988): 561-567.

Keen, Sam. *Faces of the Enemy: Reflections of the Hostile Imagination.* New York: Harper & Row, 1988.

Kelman, Herbert C. "Violence Without Moral Restraint: Reflections on the Dehumanization of Victims and their Victimizers." *Journal of Social Issues* 29 (1973): 25-61.

——— "Acknowledging the Other's Nationhood: How to Create a Momentum for the Israeli-Palestinian Negotiations." *Journal of Palestine Studies* 85 (1992): 18-38.

——— "Nationalism, Patriotism, and National Identity: Social-Psychological Dimensions." In *Patriotism: In the Lives of Individuals and Nations,* edited by D. Bar-Tal and E. Staub. Chicago: Nelson-Hall Publishers, 1997.

——— "Negotiating National Identity and Self-Determination in Ethnic Conflicts: The Choice between Pluralism and Ethnic Cleansing." *Negotiation Journal* 13 (1997): 327-340.

——— "Social-Psychological Contributions to Peacemaking and Peacebuilding in the Middle East." *Applied Psychology: An International Review* 47 (1998): 5-28.

Kelman, Herbert C., and V. Lee Hamilton. *Crimes of Obedience: Toward a Social Psychology of Authority and Responsibility.* New Haven: Yale University Press, 1989.

"Khojaly," Web site available at http://www.come.to/khojaly/, accessed February 4, 2001.

Kim, Sung Hee, and Richard H. Smith. "Revenge and Conflict Escalation." *Negotiation Journal* 9 (1993): 37-43.

Knopf, Terry Ann. *Rumors, Race, and Riots.* New Brunswick, NJ: Transaction Books, 1975.

Lachman, Sheldon J. "Psychological Perspective for a Theory of Behavior During Riots." *Psychological Reports* 79 (1996): 739-744.

"Language and Sovereignty." *Montreal Gazette,* May 9, 2000, sec. B, p. 2.

"Lanka calls for talks with Tamil Rebels." *The Times of India* (January 25, 2001). Available via the Web at: http://www.timesofindia.com/today/25nbrs2.htm

Latane, Bibb, and John M. Darley. "Group Inhibition of Bystander Intervention in Emergencies." *Journal of Personality and Social Psychology* 10 (1968): 244-268.

Le Bon, Gustave. *Psychologie des Foules* (English title *The Crowd*). With a new introduction by Robert A. Nye. New Brunswick, NJ: Transaction Books, 1995.

"Legal in English." *Montreal Gazette,* June 22, 2000, sec. B, p. 2.

LeVine, Robert A., and Donald T. Campbell. *Ethnocentrism: Theories of Conflict, Ethnic Attitudes, and Group Behavior.* New York: John Wiley & Sons, 1972.

Liberation Tigers of Tamil Eelam. "Tamil Eelam Home Page." Web page available at http://eelam.com/tamil_eelam.html, accessed January 26, 2001.

——— "The Legitimacy of the Armed Struggle of the Tamil People." Web page available at http://eelam.com/introduction/legitimacy.html, accessed January 3, 2001.

Library of Congress. "Israel—A Country Study." Available via the Web at: http://lcweb2.loc.gov/frd/cs/iltoc.html (accessed December 21, 2000).

Little, David. *Sri Lanka: The Invention of Enmity.* Washington, D.C.: United States Institute of Peace Press, 1994.

Llewellyn, John Todd. "Understanding Urban Legends: A Peculiar Public Relations Challenge." *Public Relations Quarterly* 41 (Winter 1996-1997): 17-22.

Lorenz, Konrad. *On Aggression.* Translated by Marjorie Kerr Wilson. New York: Harcourt, Brace & World, 1966.

Mack, John E. "Foreword." In V. Volkan, *Cyprus—War and Adaptation: A Psychoanalytic History of Two Ethnic Groups in Conflict.* Charlottesville, VA: University Press of Virginia, 1979.

——— "Nationalism and the Self." *The Psychohistory Review* 11(1983): 47-69.

The Mahavamsa; or, The Great Chronicle of Ceylon. Translated into English by W. Geiger. London: Pali Text Society, 1980.

Mammadova, Galina. "Larissa/Black January—January 20, 1990." *Azerbaijan International* 7 (Autumn 1999). Available via the Web at http://www.azer.com/aiweb/categories/magazine/73_folder/73_articles/73_larissa.html

Manogaran, Chelvadurai. *Ethnic Conflict and Reconciliation in Sri Lanka.* Honolulu: University of Hawaii Press, 1987.

——— "Space-Related Identity in Sri Lanka." In D. H. Kaplan and G. H. Herb, *Nested Identities: Nationalism, Territory, and Scale.* Lanham, MD: Rowman & Littlefield Publishers, Inc., 1999.

Maslow, Abraham H. "The Authoritarian Character Structure." *The Journal of Social Psychology, S.P.S.S.I. Bulletin* 18 (1943): 401-411.

——— *Toward a Psychology of Being,* 2nd ed. New York: D. Van Nostrand Company, 1968.

Matthews, Bruce. "Sinhala Cultural and Buddhist Patriotic Organizations in Contemporary Sri Lanka." *Pacific Affairs* 61 (1988): 620-632.

Mazur, A., and A. Booth. "Testosterone and Dominance in Men." *Behavioral and Brain Sciences* 21 (1998): 353-397.

McGuinness, Diane. "Introduction: The Function of Status and Rank in Inter-Male Aggression and War." In *Dominance, Aggression, and War,* edited by D. McGuinness. New York: Paragon House Publishers, 1987.

McKay, Matthew, Patrick Fanning, Carole Honeychurch, and Catherine Sutker. *The Self-Esteem Companion: Simple Exercises to Help You Challenge Your Inner Critic and Celebrate Your Personal Strengths.* Oakland, CA: New Harbinger Publications, Inc., 1999.

Montville, Joseph V. "The Healing Function in Political Conflict Resolution." In D. J. D. Sandole and H. van der Merwe, eds., *Conflict Resolution Theory and Practice: Integration and Application.* Manchester: Manchester University Press, 1993.

Morrow, Lance. "Unspeakable Crimes." *Time* (February 22, 1993): 48-50.

Moyer, K. E. "The Biological Basis of Dominance and Aggression." In *Dominance, Aggression, and War,* edited by D. McGuinness. New York: Paragon House Publishers, 1987.

National Movement Against Terrorism. "The Gonagala Massacre by the LTTE." Colombo: National Movement Against Terrorism, no date.

Nelson, Susan L. *Healing the Broken Heart: Sin, Alienation, and the Gift of Grace.* St. Louis: Chalice Press, 1997.

Neumann, Erich. *Depth Psychology and a New Ethic.* Translated by E. Rolfe. New York: G. P. Putnam's Sons, 1969 (original work published 1949).

Nolyain, Igor. "Moscow's Initiation of the Azeri-Armenian Conflict." *Central Asian Survey* 13 (1994): 541-563.

Obeyesekere, Gannath. "Sinhalese-Buddhist Identity in Ceylon." In *Ethnic Identity: Cultural Continuities and Change,* edited by G. de Vos and L. Romanucci-Ross. Palo Alto, CA: Mayfield Publishing Company, 1988.

Oette, Lutz. *The International Crime of Genocide: The Case of the Tamil People in Sri Lanka.* London: Tamil Information Centre, 1997.

O'Neill, Juliet. "No Massacre Took Place, Armenia says; Victims Were Used as Cover During Fight, Authorities Say." *The Vancouver Sun* (March 6, 1992): A10.

Perera, Jehan. "An Analysis of the Breakdown of Negotiations in the Sri Lankan Ethnic Conflict." In K. Rupesinghe (ed.), *Negotiating Peace in Sri Lanka: Efforts, Failures, and Lessons.* London: International Alert, 1998.

Perlez, Jane, and David E. Sanger. "White House Says It Sees Some Hope to End Standoff." *The New York Times* (April 6, 2001): A1.

Pfaffenberger, Bryan. "Ethnic Conflict and Youth Insurgency in Sri Lanka: The Social Origins of Tamil Separatism." In *Conflict and Peacemaking in Multiethnic Societies,* edited by J. V. Montville. Lexington, MA: Lexington Books, 1991.

Pirabakaran, Velupillai. "2000 Heroes' Day Message." Posted as a press release by Eelam House in London. Accessed via the Web at http://eelam.com/freedom_struggle/ltte_press_releases/2000/november/27.html, November 29, 2000.

Ponsonby, Arthur. *Falsehood in War-Time: Containing an Assortment of Lies Circulated Throughout the Nations During the Great War.* New York: E. P. Dutton & Co., Inc., 1928.

Pratkanis, Anthony R., and Elliot Aronson. *Age of Propaganda: The Everyday Use and Abuse of Persuasion.* New York: W. H. Freeman, 1992.

Pruitt, Dean G., and Jeffrey Z. Rubin. *Social Conflict: Escalation, Stalemate, and Settlement.* New York: Random House, 1986.

Quattrone, George, and E. E. Jones. "The Perception of Variability Within Ingroups and Out-groups: Implications for the Law of Small Numbers." *Journal of Personality and Social Psychology* 38 (1980): 141-152.

Ra'anan, Uri. "The Nation-State Fallacy." In *Conflict and Peacemaking in Multiethnic Societies* (pp. 5-20), edited by J. V. Montville. Lexington, MA: Lexington Books, 1991.

Rahula, Walpola Sri. *What the Buddha Taught* (Revised Edition). New York: Grove Press, 1974.

Rajanayagam, P. "Government–LTTE Negotiations (1994–1995): Another Lost Opportunity." In K. Rupesinghe (ed.), *Negotiating Peace in Sri Lanka: Efforts, Failures, and Lessons*. London: International Alert, 1998.

Read, James Morgan. *Atrocity Propaganda 1914-1919*. New Haven, CT: Yale University Press, 1941.

Renwick, Neil, and Qing Cao. "China's Political Discourse Towards the 21st Century: Victimhood, Identity, and Political Power." *East Asia: An International Quarterly* 17 (1999), 111ff.

Richler, Mordecai. *Oh Canada! Oh Quebec!: Requiem for a Divided Country*. New York: A. A. Knopf, 1992.

Rogers, Carl R. *On Becoming a Person: A Therapist's View of Psychotherapy*. New York: Houghton Mifflin, 1995 (original work published 1961).

——— *The Carl Rogers Reader*. Edited by H. Kirschenbaum and V. L. Henderson. Boston: Houghton Mifflin Company, 1989.

Rogers, John D., Jonathan Spencer, and Jayadeva Uyangoda. "Sir Lanka: Political Violence and Ethnic Conflict." *American Psychologist* 53 (1998): 771-777.

Rosnow, Ralph L., and Gary Alan Fine. *Rumor and Gossip: The Social Psychology of Hearsay*. New York: Elsevier, 1976.

Rothbart, Myron, M. Evans, and S. Fulero. "Recall for Confirming Events: Memory Processes and the Maintenance of Social Stereotypes." *Journal of Experimental Social Psychology* 15 (1979), 343-355.

Rupesinghe, Kumar (Ed.). *Negotiating Peace in Sri Lanka: Efforts, Failures, and Lessons*. London: International Alert, 1998.

Russell, Gordon W. "Personalities in the Crowd: Those Who Would Escalate a Sports Riot." *Aggressive Behaivor* 21 (1995): 91-100.

"Rwanda: Genocidal Rape Conviction." *Off Our Backs* 29 (1999): 4.

Sangam Research U.S.A. "Kosovo (before NATO) and Tamil Eelam," (1999). Pamphlet available from Ilankai Tamil Sangam at e-mail address: secretary@sangam.org

Seneca. *Thyestes* (American Philological Association Textbook Series #11). Edited by R. J. Tarrant. Atlanta: Scholars Press, 1985.

Shahmuratian, Samvel (Ed.). *The Sumgait Tragedy: Pogroms Against Armenians in Soviet Azerbaijan, Volume I: Eyewitness Accounts*. Cambridge: The Zoryan Institute, 1990.

Shastri, Amita. "The Material Basis for Separatism: The Tamil Eelam Movement in Sri Lanka." *The Journal of Asian Studies* 49 (1990): 56-77.

Shaw, R. Paul, and Yuwa Wong. *Genetic Seeds of Warfare: Evolution, Nationalism, and Patriotism*. Boston: Unwin Hyman, 1989.

Sherif, Muzafer. *In Common Predicament: Social Psychology of Intergroup Conflict and Cooperation*. Boston: Houghton Mifflin, 1966.

Shibutani, Tamotsu. *Improvised News: A Sociological Study of Rumor*. Indianapolis, IN: The Bobbs-Merrill Company, Inc, 1966.

Shinkwba, Bagrat, and others. "Appeal to the Russian Writers' Union, Writers' Organisations of the CIS States, the North Caucasian Republics, Tataria,

Bashkortostan, Near Eastern Countries: Lebanon, Syria, Jordan, Egypt; of America, Turkey, England, Germany, France, Poland, Czech Republic, Hungary, Baltic Republics and other States." Web page available at http://www.abkhazia.org/writers.html, accessed January 3, 2001.

Shnirelman, Victor A. *Who Gets the Past? Competition for Ancestors among Non-Russian Intellectuals in Russia.* Washington, D.C.: The Woodrow Wilson Center Press, 1996.

Shweder, R. A., and E. J. Bourne. "Does the Concept of the Person Vary Cross-Culturally?" In *Culture Theory: Essays on Mind, Self, and Emotion,* edited by R. A. Shweder and R. A. LeVine. Cambridge, U.K.: Cambridge University Press, 1984.

Sieghart, Paul. *Sri Lanka—A Mounting Tragedy of Errors* (Report of a Mission to Sri Lanka in January 1984 on behalf of the International Commission of Jurists and its British Section, JUSTICE). London: International Commission of Jurists/JUSTICE, 1984.

Sihala Urumaya. "Sihala Urumaya to Help Crush Terrorism." Web page available at http://sihalaurumaya.s5.com/SUto%20crush.htm, accessed January 22, 2001.

Singer, Marshall R. "Prospects for Conflict Management in the Sri Lankan Ethnic Crisis." In *Conflict and Peacemaking in Multiethnic Societies,* edited by J. M. Montville. Lexington, MA: Lexington Books, 1991.

Sisk, Timothy D. (Ed.). *New Approaches to International Negotiation and Mediation: Findings from USIP-Sponsored Research.* Washington, D.C.: United States Institute of Peace, 1999.

Smith, Anthony D. *National Identity.* London: Penguin Books, 1991.

Smith, Craig S. "U.S. and China Look for a Way to Say 'Sorry': Right Apology Depends on Its Interpretation." *The New York Times* (April 9, 2001): A1.

———— "China Releases U.S. Plane Crew 11 Days After Midair Collision: Envoy 'Very Sorry'." *The New York Times* (April 12, 2001): A1.

Solomon, Robert C. *A Passion for Justice: Emotions and the Origins of the Social Contract.* Reading, MA: Addison-Wesley Pub. Co., 1990.

Specter, Michael. "Zhirinovsky and the Motherland." *The New York Times Magazine* (June 19, 1994): 28-56.

Staub, Ervin. *The Roots of Evil: The Origins of Genocide and Other Group Violence.* Cambridge, U.K.: Cambridge University Press, 1989.

———— "Cultural-Societal Roots of Violence: The Examples of Genocidal Violence and of Contemporary Youth Violence in the United States." *American Psychologist* 51 (1996): 117-132.

Stott, Clifford, and Steve Reicher. "How Conflict Escalates: The Inter-group Dynamics of Collective Football Crowd Violence." *Sociology* 32 (1998): 353-378.

Stout, Maureen. *The Feel-Good Curriculum: The Dumbing-Down of America's Kids in the Name of Self-Esteem.* Cambridge, MA: Perseus Books, 2000.

Sumner, William Graham. *Folkways: A Study of the Sociological Importance of Usages, Manners, Customs, Mores, and Morals.* Boston: Ginn & Company, 1940 (original work published 1906).

Suny, Ronald Grigor. *Looking Toward Ararat: Armenia in Modern History.* Blooming-ton: Indiana University Press, 1993.

———— *The Revenge of the Past: Nationalism, Revolution, and the Collapse of the Soviet Union.* Stanford, CA: Stanford University Press, 1993.

Swiss, Shana, Peggy J. Jennings, Gladys V. Aryee, Grace H. Brown, Ruth M. Jappah-Samukai, Mary S. Kamara, Rosana D. H. Schaack, and Rujatu S. Turay-Kanneh. "Violence against Women During the Liberian Civil Conflict (Letter from Monrovia)." *JAMA, The Journal of the American Medical Association* 279 (February 25, 1998): 625-630.

Tajfel, Henri. *Human Groups and Social Categories: Studies in Social Psychology.* Cam-bridge, U.K.: Cambridge University Press, 1981.

Tajfel, Henri, and John C. Turner. "The Social Identity Theory of Intergroup Behavior." In *Psychology of Intergroup Relations,* edited by S. Worschel and W. G. Austin. Chicago: Nelson-Hall Publishers, 1986.

Tambiah, Stanley J. *Sri Lanka: Ethnic Fratricide and the Dismantling of Democracy.* Chicago: The University of Chicago Press, 1986.

———— *Leveling Crowds: Ethnonationalist Conflicts and Collective Violence in South Asia.* Berkeley: The University of California Press, 1996.

———— "Friends, Neighbors, Enemies, Strangers: Aggressor and Victim in Civilian Ethnic Riots." *Social Science and Medicine* 45 (1997): 1177-1188.

TamilCanadian. "Destruction of Jaffna Public Library." Web page available at: http://www.tamilcanadian.com/eelam/hrights/html/article/SU980516114546N30.html. Accessed December 27, 2000.

"Tamil Inmates Butchered in Sri Lanka Open Prison, Toll 25." 123India.com: News: Regional, Oct 25, 2000. Accessed via the Web at http://www.123India.com, October 30, 2000.

Tillich, Paul. *The Shaking of the Foundations.* New York: C. Scribner's Sons, 1950.

———— *The Courage to Be.* New Haven, CT: Yale University Press, 1952.

Trevor-Roper, Hugh. "The Invention of Tradition: The Highland Tradition of Scotland." In E. Hobsbawm and T. Ranger (eds.), *The Invention of Tradition.* Cambridge, U.K.: Cambridge University Press, 1992.

Triandis, Harry C. *Individualism and Collectivism.* Boulder, CO: Westview Press, 1995.

Tulviste, Peeter. "History Taught at School Versus History Discovered at Home: The Case of Estonia." *European Journal of Psychology of Education* 9 (1994): 121-126.

Turner, John C. "Social Comparison and Social Identity: Some Prospects for Inter-group Behaviour." *European Journal of Social Psychology* 5 (1975), 5-34.

Turner, John C., Penelope J. Oakes, S. Alexander Haslam, and Craig McGarty. "Self and Collective: Cognition and Social Context." *Personality and Social Psychology Bulletin* 20 (1994): 454-463.

"The Uses and Abuses of History." *The Economist* (December 21, 1996): 71-74.

United States Department of State. "Erasing History: Ethnic Cleansing in Kosovo." Report released by the U.S. Department of State, Washington, D.C., May 1999. Available via the Web at http://www.state.gov/www/regions/eur/rpt_9905_ethnic_ksvo_toc.html, accessed December 28, 2000.

Van Langenhove, Fernand. *The Growth of a Legend: A Study Based upon the German Accounts of Francs-Tireurs and "Atrocities" in Belgium.* Translated by E. B. Sherlock. New York: G. P. Putnam's Sons, 1916.

Vaserman, Arie, and Rami Ginat. "National, Territorial or Religious Conflict? The Case of Nagorno-Karabakh." *Studies in Conflict and Terrorism* 17(1994): 345-362.

Volkan, Vamik. *Cyprus—War and Adaptation: A Psychoanalytic History of Two Ethnic Groups in Conflict.* Charlottesville: University Press of Virginia, 1979.

——— "Psychoanalytic Aspects of Ethnic Conflicts." In *Conflict and Peacemaking in Multiethnic Societies,* edited by J. V. Montville. Lexington, MA: Lexington Books, 1991.

——— *The Need to Have Enemies and Allies: From Clinical Practice to International Relationships.* Northvale, NJ: Jason Aronson, 1994.

Wertsch, James V. "Narrative Tools of History and Identity." *Culture & Psychology* 3 (1997): 5-20.

——— *Voices of Collective Remembering.* Cambridge, U.K.: Cambridge University Press, 2001.

"Who Wants a Separate State?" A Publication of the Ministry of State, The Government of Sri Lanka, Overseas Information Series, No. 9. Accessed via the Web at: http://ourworld.compuserve.com/homepages/sinhala/, September 13, 2000.

Worchel, Stephen. *Written in Blood: Ethnic Identity and the Struggle for Human Harmony.* New York: Worth Publishing, 1998.

Zimbardo, Philip G. "The Human Choice: Individuation, Reason, and Order Versus Deindividuation." In W. J. Arnold and D. Levine, eds., *Nebraska Symposium on Motivation* 17 (1969): 237-307.

INDEX